Cardinal Mazarin

Arthur Hassall

Published 2016 by Ozymandias Press

CONTENTS

THE EARLY YEARS OF
MAZARIN'S MINISTRY

Richelieu died on the 5th of December 1642; on the following day Louis XIII. announced that he had chosen Mazarin to be First Minister. Giulio Mazarini, or Jules Mazarin, as the French call him, was born on July 14, 1602, at Piscina, a small village in the Abruzzi. His father was a certain Sicilian, by name Pietro Mazarini, his mother was Hortensia Buffalini, who was renowned for her beauty. To the latter the young Giulio owed much of his future success, for it was due to her efforts that he first studied under the Jesuits at the Roman College, and later at the University of Alcalá in Spain. He had early shown signs of uncommon talents, and he was at the age of sixteen remarkable for his.handsome face and natural brightness. On his return to Rome about the year 1622, he entered the pontifical army, only to find that his real *métier* was diplomacy. He had studied civil law and had taken his degree of doctor *in utroque jure,* and under Cardinals Barberini and Sachetti he plunged into the tangled maze of Italian politics. Service under the Pope gave him an unrivalled opportunity of making himself acquainted with the political state of Europe, and of practising that adroitness and persuasiveness which proved so valuable when he became First Minister in France. Idleness was never one of his faults, and during these years in the service of his master at the Vatican Mazarin showed himself indefatigable, subtle, and successful. By his patience and industry he soon acquired an insight into diplomatic mysteries, and till the end of his life was pre-eminently a diplomatist of the first order. His ability was fully recognised by the Cardinals Barberini and Sachetti, and the war of the Mantuan succession brought him into contact with Richelieu.

On March 30,1630, the French had captured Pinerolo, the fortress commanding the exit of the chief pass from Dauphiné into Italy. The Spaniards and Imperialists offered to negotiate, and Mazarin, who was employed as papal legate, attracted the notice of the French cardinal. The negotiations came to nothing, as Richelieu refused to yield Pinerolo. When, later in the year, Cásale, besieged by Spinola, was hard pressed, Mazarin, in the absence of Richelieu, who had returned to France, arranged a truce at Rivalta on September 4, very much to the advantage of the beleaguered garrison, it is not to be wondered at that Richelieu should have decided to secure the services of the young Mazarin, for whom he procured a cardinal's hat. Richelieu's confidence in his protégé was not misplaced, and on his death-bed he recommended Mazarin to Louis as his successor.

Before, however, Mazarin could establish himself firmly in power, and continue and complete his predecessor's policy, Louis XIII. died, and an opportunity was given for an outbreak of all the discontent which had been seething in France during Richelieu's later years. Louis died on May 14, 1643; on May 18 the *parlement* of Paris, anticipating the action of its successor in 1715 on the death of Louis XIV., abolished the council which by the will of the late king had been set up, placed the supreme power in the hands of the queen-mother, Anne of Austria, an easy-natured but at the same time a proud and capable woman, and appointed Gaston, Duke of Orleans—a mere puppet in the hands of any strong man—lieutenant-general of the kingdom. This conduct of the *parlement,* and the attitude which it adopted, Vas due to the belief of its members that their political influence would be restored, that Mazarin would retire to Italy, and that the whole policy of Richelieu would be reversed. The *parlement* had thus modified the will of the late king, and had organised the regency. It had, in a word, returned again to political life, from which in 1641 it had been most carefully excluded by Richelieu ; and during the greater portion of Louis XIV.'s minority it played a prominent part in the politics of the time. But its pretensions were odious to the queen-mother and to Mazarin, who, while endeavouring till the outbreak of the Fronde to preserve internal peace, was always jealous of any attacks on the royal prerogative. In her attitude of constant watchfulness over her son's rights Anne was ever loyally supported by the cardinal, whom the *parlement* regarded with reason as its principal foe. The *parlement* had expected that Anne would prove pliable and carry out its wishes. Before long, however, the queen-mother definitely indicated the position which, as regent, she intended to adopt, and from that moment the rift between the *parlement* and the government became deeper and deeper.

On the evening of May 18, the queen-mother announced a decision which proved to be a momentous one in the history of the French monarchy. Mazarin was confirmed in his position as First Minister, and the hopes of the *parlement* were disappointed. The work of consolidating the French monarchy was not to be interrupted, and the policy of humbling the Austro-Spanish house was to be continued.

Hatred of Richelieu as First Minister had been general among the noble class during the greater part of Louis XIII.'s reign. Anne's announcement presaged the continuance of a system of government which was odious to the feudal as well as to the legal aristocracy. The disaffected, therefore, at once resolved to resist the rule of Mazarin, and a system of uncompromising opposition to the supremacy of an Italian adventurer was organised.

The situation of France was at this time extremely critical. Richelieu's death already had disastrous effects on the military administration, and energetic action on the part of the government was necessary. Ammunition was deficient, supplies of all kinds were with difficulty forthcoming, and the bonds of discipline had been seriously relaxed. While the ranks were weakened by frequent desertions, general officers had left their respective posts, and many of the subalterns were absent from their duty. It seemed very doubtful if the army of the North would be able to take the field. Equally serious had been the effects of the death of the great cardinal on the stability of the government. Many persons imprisoned or exiled by Richelieu now returned to Paris, and were ready to avenge their wrongs on his successor. Anxious to secure pensions .and offices, they were wanting in political responsibility, and cared nothing for the welfare of France. The return of these exiles rendered Mazarin's position unspeakably difficult, and forced him for a time to adopt a policy of compromise.

The issue was, however, plain. Was the work of crushing the great nobles, and of making French influence supreme on the Continent, to be continued? Was the French monarchy to symbolise the unity of France? Mazarin embodied the continuance and development of Richelieu's policy. He consistently aimed at abolishing feudalism and making the monarchy supreme. Consequently, he at once became the object of bitter attacks. All those who disapproved of Richelieu's policy immediately ranged themselves in opposition to Mazarin, and resolved to abolish the post of First Minister. For some ten years the internal development of France was checked, while the feudal and legal aristocracies endeavoured to regain their lost positions, to reverse the foreign policy of the last two reigns, and to destroy Mazarin. In consequence of the cessation of Richelieu's drastic methods the nobles and *parlement* did succeed in plunging France into confusion, and by their action fully justified the measures by which they were ultimately suppressed. The new policy of leniency and concession in place of that of stern repression was, however, seen after a few years to have failed in every respect ; but it was not till 1653 that Mazarin was able to remedy the evil results of the easy rule of Anne of

Austria from 1643 to 1648, and of his own neglect of the internal administration.

Mazarin, during the first years of his ministry, found himself in a very difficult position. Unlike Richelieu, who was supported by the king, Mazarin could only rely upon a woman and a child ; and Anne of Austria, by her good-nature and desire to satisfy everybody, made a stern policy for the time impossible. Opposed to him were "powerful rivals and redoubtable enemies," and while he had the management of the kingdom placed in his hands, his work was continually hampered by the acts of the queen-mother's friends, who, hitherto exiled and disgraced, were returning in large numbers to France. Fortunately he was able to unravel the various plots formed against him in France, while his intimate acquaintance with the political state of Europe stood him in good stead in directing the foreign policy of the kingdom. Before the first surprise occasioned by the confirmation of Mazarin in his post as First Minister had worn off came the news of the decisive victory of Rocroi. Nothing could have happened more opportunely for the minister. The government was strengthened, its enemies confounded, and the early years of the reign opened in brilliant fashion. Mazarin had fortunately confirmed the Duke of Enghien, son of Prince Henry of Condé, in the command of the army of the North. His genius for war not being at the time generally known, the veteran l'Hôpital was chosen to guide and control his actions. On assuming the command, Enghien's ascendency was at once felt. He restored the discipline and confidence of the army and made preparations for taking the offensive. The Spanish army, however, under Mello, forestalled his intentions, and as a preliminary to the invasion of France, and to a march upon Paris by the valleys of the Marne and the Aisne, the Spanish general besieged the small fortress of Rocroi. Putting aside l'Hôpital's plea for caution, Enghien, ably supported by Grassion, a cavalry leader of great promise, rapidly advanced, and on May 19, 1643, the famous battle of Rocroi was fought. The Spanish army, which included many Italians and AValloons, numbered 27,000, against tlieir opponent's 23,000. At first the French left wing was driven back and the victory of Spain seemed assured. But Enghien's dash and skill restored the fortunes of the day, and he won a decisive victory over the renowned and experienced troops opposed to him. For the first time in a hundred years, Spain suffered a defeat at the hands of France.

Until the fatal day of Blenheim the ascendency of French arms in Europe was established. Thionville was at once besieged, and, owing to Enghien's engineering skill, surrendered on August 18. These successes strengthened the hands of the minister and enabled him to deal an overwhelming blow at the cabal of the *Importants,* who, headed by the Duke of Beaufort, were conspiring to bring about his downfall.

The conspirators—who included the Duchess of Chevreuse, Richelieu's old enemy and the most famous political schemer of the day ; the Bishop of Beauvais, an intriguer of the first water, "the most idiot of idiots"; Montrésor, " who had the outside of a Cato, but none of his virtues " ; the Duchess of Montbazon and the beautiful Duchess of Longueville, two clever and unscrupulous court ladies; the Duke of Beaufort; and the rascally Abbé de la Rivière — had determined to play upon Anne of Austria's good-nature, to destroy Richelieu's system and change his policy, and, in a word, to seize the government. Mazarin himself was alive to the hatred which pursued Richelieu's memory, and counselled toleration of all opinions. "Time," he wrote, "will avenge that great man of all these insults, and those who blame him to-day will find out hereafter, perhaps, how much his guidance would have been necessary to complete the happiness of the realm—the happiness of which he has laid the foundation. Let us then suffer the malice of ignorant and prejudiced minds to evaporate freely, since opposition will only serve to irritate it." These broad - minded views failed to conciliate the *Importants,* and when the Duchess of Montbazon was exiled for insulting the queen, Beaufort resolved to have the cardinal assassinated. The plot failed, and on September 2 Beaufort was arrested, and the *Importants* virtually ceased to exist. This vigorous action on the part of the government was received with general satisfaction. "The whole population," wrote Mazarin, "was overjoyed." It was now clearly manifest that, though Mazarin's courtesy and gentleness bore a striking contrast to the domineering manner of his predecessor, Richelieu himself was no less resolute than the Italian cardinal. Men recognised that Richelieu's mantle had indeed descended on Mazarin. "Il n'est pas mort : il n'a que changé d'âge," was the first line of a rondeau composed after the *coup d'état* of September 2, 1643, in which it was wittily suggested that Mazarin was Richelieu himself.

Though the cardinal was now firmly established in

power, and supported at court by many devoted friends, such as Antoine, Marshal of Gramont, René-Potier, the Count of Tresmes, Roger du Plessis, the Marquis of Liancourt, and others, he had many serious difficulties to face. The Duke of Orleans and the Condé family were mutually jealous and desirous of securing important provincial governments. Henry Condé demanded Languedoc for himself and the estates of Chantilly and Dammartin,—in fact, the whole of the domains of his brother-in-law, Henry of Montmorency. Enghien was to have Burgundy; and as the Duke of Longueville, Condé's son-in-law, was governor of Normandy, it was evident that acquiescence with demands such as these would prove highly detrimental to the development of the French monarchy. Orleans, on his part, demanded Champagne with Sedan. Cardinal Bichi had advised Mazarin to bring about an understanding between Orleans and Henry Condé, and to rule by their means. Mazarin, however, made no attempt to carry out this suggestion. He preferred the safer plan of playing them off the one against the other; and for carrying out this policy he was by nature remarkably well suited. By giving Languedoc, on which Condé had set his heart, to Orleans, he preserved the friendship of the latter and stirred up strife between the two families. All through the year 1643 the provincial question had occupied his mind. The increase in taxation, and the severity and dishonesty of the methods of collecting taxes, had caused great discontent in the country districts, and in the autumn of 1643 the peasants of Rouergue rose, and their example was shortly afterwards imitated by the people in Lower Poitou, Saintonge, and the Angoumois. Langeron, to whom had been committed the duty of suppressing the rising, after meeting with serious resistance, put down the revolt in Rouergue with an armed force; but in the other districts the nobles themselves took part in the risings, and a state of things somewhat similar to that then existing in England was created. A small army was promptly sent to the disturbed districts, but measures of severity were rarely employed, and a general amnesty was granted. By this mixture of firmness in suppressing disorder and of humanity in sparing the people, Mazarin succeeded by the beginning of 1644 in restoring order in the provinces. Like the Norman kings, Mazarin had fully realised that it was politic to be generous to the mass of the nation, who would be, if well governed, a source of wealth to the crown. " The queen's absolute intention," he wrote to the *intendant* of Languedoc, " is that every possible facility may be given to the people to pay the subventions which the inevitable necessity of public affairs compels Her Majesty to require from them." Meanwhile other but not less effective measures were being taken to ensure the stability of the government. Believing that the influence of the episcopacy was used against him, and fearing lest the queen should be affected by it, Mazarin ordered some sixty-two bishops to return from Paris to their dioceses. The cardinal's triumph over the nobles, the bishops, and the court ladies was due in great measure to his personal influence with the queen. At the time the strength of this influence was never suspected, and Mazarin's fall was confidently anticipated. The secret of this influence was for two centuries a source of difficulty, but from Michelet's time historians of high authority have accepted the view that Mazarin and Anne of Austria were united by marriage. Mazarin had early gained not only the admiration, but also the affection of the queen-regent. To this affection was due the fidelity with which Anne adhered to the fortunes of the cardinal during the whole of the Fronde period. To this affection were due the earlier and later triumphs of Mazarin. Being only in deacon's orders, Mazarin, though a cardinal, could lawfully marry.

So far the anxieties of the government had been the natural outcome of the changes consequent upon the deaths of Richelieu and Louis XIII. The initial difficulties of the new reign had been overcome and the rule of Anne of Austria and of Mazarin had been apparently firmly established. It remained to bring the war to a successful conclusion. To effect this desirable end, large supplies of money were absolutely necessary. Richelieu had left the finances in a desperate condition. The system of farming the taxes was a most ruinous one, and it was only by borrowing at an exorbitant rate of interest that funds could be procured. In 1644 the expenditure had risen from 99,000,000 livres in 1642 to 124,000,000, of which 59,000,000 never reached the treasury. It was necessary to raise money, and during the contests of the government with the *parlement* of Paris not only were the glaring defects of the French financial system made apparent, but many points of comparison between the situation in England and that in France could be observed.

Early in 1644 Particelli d'Emery, the dishonest controller-general of finance, imposed a tax of forty sous on every *toise* of land built upon, outside the walls of Paris. The inhabitants affected appealed to the *parlement,* and a contest arose between that body and the government. Simultaneously in the provinces riots took place against the imposition of certain taxes. The danger of a general uprising all over the country was a real one, and before it the government recoiled. It was resolved to withdraw the edict of the *toisé,* and to substitute a *taxe des aises* which would not fall on the poorer classes. By this tax Emery expected to obtain about forty millions. But the *parlement,* on the suggestion of Omer Talon, the advocate-general, demanded that the whole of the legal class should be exempted from the operation of this measure. As many others also obtained exemption, it resulted that upon the farmers of the revenue would fall the full force of the exaction. This necessary but unpopular class at once raised a great outcry. If they were abandoned by the court they would no longer furnish the required supplies. The public credit would be ruined and the government would be helpless. Recognising that the numerous exceptions had destroyed the utility of the tax, Emery at once withdrew it, and in March 1645 reimposed the *toisé.* The opposition which this measure provoked was so violent that Anne arrested and exiled some of the members of the *parlement.* In an interview held previously, Anne had silenced the President Gayant with the words, " Taisezvous ; je vous connais vieux fou." In spite of the energy shown by the government, Mazarin recognised the existence of deep discontent in the country. Had it not been for the victory of Enghien and Turenne at Nördlingen in August 1645, an early outbreak of the Fronde might have taken place. The victory, however, enabled the court to adopt a bold attitude, and Mazarin hoped that other successes such as that won at Nördlingen would enable him to make a satisfactory peace, to be followed by the establishment of order and prosperity in France.

After the Rocroi and Thionville campaign, a force under Rantzau had penetrated into Germany, where it was defeated at Düttlingen by Mercy, the Austrian general. That reverse was, however, compensated for by the French success in three desperate battles at Freiburg in 1644, where Turenne and Condé both showed great skill By the end of 1644 French armies were in occupation of the Rhine Valley. In 1645 Turenne, like Villars in the Spanish Succession War, made an attempt to unite with the Swedes in a concerted advance upon Vienna. Ragotsky, Prince of Transylvania, had been won over by Mazarin, and had engaged to aid the Swedish general Torstenson, while Turenne marched on Vienna through Swabia. Unfortunately for the success of the scheme,'Turenne, on May 5, 1645, was defeated at Mergentheim, and Torstenson was incapacitated by illness. Reinforced by Enghien and eight thousand men, Turenne avenged the check which he had received by aiding his brilliant colleague to win the battle of Nördlingen on August 3. In this desperate struggle, in which both sides suffered heavily, Mercy was killed ; but so severe were the French losses that, though the road to Vienna lay open, Turenne was unable to advance. Moreover, as Ragotsky and Torstenson, who had recovered from his illness, had both retreated, and as Enghien was ill, it would have been folly to have moved forward with a weakened force. As it was, however, the reputation of the French arms was fully re-established, and the hands of the opposition, exultant after Mergentheim, were weakened.

A few days after the battle of Nördlingen, Mazarin had achieved a valuable diplomatic success. Since the beginning of 1644 Sweden and Denmark had been at war—the result of Austrian intrigues at Copenhagen. Torstenson and Horn thereupon invaded Denmark, leaving France to bear the weight of the struggle in Germany. This diversion of the Swedish forces tended to prolong the war against the Hapsburgs, and Mazarin hastened to intervene at Copenhagen and Stockholm in favour of peace. He was supported by the presence of a Dutch fleet in the Baltic ; preliminaries of peace were signed at the end of the year 1644, and Torstenson returned to Germany with his troops. Under the mediation of the French ambassador, la Thuillerie, conferences between the Danish and Swedish envoys were opened at Brömsebro. Influenced by the successes of the Swedes in Germany and Bohemia, where, in April, Torstenson defeated the Austrians at Jankowitz, and by the determination of the Dutch to support Sweden, Christian IV. of Denmark consented to the proposed terms, and on August 14, 1645, the Treaty of Brömsebro was signed. France had not only brought about peace, but had secured definite territorial advantages for her ally. At the same time Mazarin recognised the advantage of conciliating Denmark, and on November 25, 1645, he made a treaty with that power advantageous to French commerce. He also endeavoured to strengthen the French alliance with Poland and Transylvania, and spared no pains to gain for France the position of protectress of the German princes and German liberties. The military successes of Turenne and Enghien in Germany, of Gassion and Rantzau in Flanders, and of Harcourt and of la Mothe-Houdancourt in Spain, tended to place France in the first rank among the European powers. This position had been won by an unpopular Italian cardinal, who, while conducting complicated negotiations, and superintending distant military operations, was engaged at home in a continuous struggle with a violent and unpatriotic opposition, and with increasing financial difficulties. Taking advantage of the victory of Nördlingen, Mazarin determined to strike a blow at the opposition without delay.

On September 7, 1645, a few weeks after Nördlingen, a *lit de justice* was held. The *parlement* adopted a submissive tone and registered nineteen financial edicts, creating many new offices and taxing various trades ; while the government wisely withdrew the *toisé* and the *taxe des aises*. Mazarin had triumphed, but his triumph was mainly due to the opportune victory of Nördlingen. This success gave the government three years of breathing-time, during which the opposition of the *parlement* to the minister increased. For the moment, however, Mazarin had won a distinct success. His power increased, and he was given the duty of super-intending the education of the young king. In spite of his momentary triumph over his enemies, the opposition to the minister grew steadily during the years succeeding the battle of Nördlingen. Mazarin was continually attacked both openly and covertly by his enemies. Even Orleans, influenced by such men as Louis d'Astarac, the Marquis of Fontrailles, one of the most dangerous characters of the day, and by the ambitious Duchess of Montbazon, took up an attitude of opposition, which, while not a serious danger, tended further to increase the difficulties of the government.

More dangerous was the hostility of Henry of Condé. His hatred of Mazarin had never ceased, and he now took advantage of the battle of Nördlingen to demand for his son Enghien the sovereignty of Charleville-sur-Meuse. On Mazarin's refusal, Condé took every opportunity, in conjunction with the Count of Chavigny, to oppose and hamper the minister. At the same time Paul Gondi, coadjutor of his uncle, the Archbishop of Paris, began his celebrated career of hostility to Mazarin and to the French government. Richelieu would have cut short these numberless intrigues by arrests and executions : Mazarin met them by dissimulation. An adept himself in the art of intrigue, he eventually defeated his enemies with their own weapons. But the opposition was so widespread, and had now, by the leniency of the government, been allowed to become so powerful, that there is little doubt that, in spite of Nördlingen and other victories, Mazarin would have been driven from France had he not continued to possess the full confidence and affection of the queen-regent. If, as has been taken for granted, the cardinal and Anne of Austria were united by a secret marriage, it is easy to explain the constant support which Mazarin received from Anne. In 1646 the intrigues continued. The French, on June 14, had been defeated at Orbitello, and the defeat had given the signal for renewed attacks on the minister ; while Enghien's capture of Dunkirk later in the year, so far from strengthening the government, only served to render more emphatic the contrast between the plans of the minister and those of the general. Attacks on Mazarin and the queen were circulated : the period of Mazarinades had definitely begun. Ignoring these anonymous publications, Mazarin now took steps to check his enemies. Orleans, who 'had returned to Paris in September 1646, after the capture of

Mardyke, was not again given a command ; Henry of Condé was treated with quiet contempt, and not allowed any active share in the administration.

The siege of Mardyke was only an operation preliminary to the more important siege of Dunkirk. Mazarin's heart was set on its capture, which he hoped would prove to be the first step towards the conquest of the Spanish Netherlands. He spared no pains to attain success. He conciliated Enghien ; he increased the army in Flanders by recruits from Ireland, Scotland, and Poland. To his expenditure of time and money was due the fall of Dunkirk, for without Mazarin's elaborate preparations Enghien's brilliant military qualities could have effected nothing. The majority of the leading officers in the French army regarded the enterprise as hopeless, but Mazarin never lost heart, and his views were readily accepted by Enghien, whose optimism was usually justified. Mazarin rightly attached great importance to the action of the Dutch. A diversion by the stadtholder would have most beneficial results, and a large portion of the Spanish army would be held in check. Unfortunately, the stadtholder fell ill at the moment, but after some delay the States-General decided to take the offensive, and, as Mazarin had anticipated, a portion of the Spanish forces was detached to watch the Dutch. In September 1646 Dunkirk was isolated. The Dutch fleet under Tromp prevented any reinforcements from entering the port of Dunkirk, and Tromp was joined by fifteen French ships. The Spaniards were helpless. To the English parliament they appealed for aid, but England was in the throes of civil war and neither party could spare troops to assist Spain. The success of Mazarin's foreign policy during these years was in great measure due to the continuance of the Civil War in England. One of the cardinal points of English policy was to watch with jealousy any advance of the French towards Flanders. Had England been under a settled government, there is no doubt effective aid would have been given to the Spaniards, and Dunkirk would not have fallen into French hands. As it was, the English parliament, though much excited at the prospect of the French capture of Dunkirk, could do nothing, and Enghien pressed on his attacks upon the town. Its governor, the Marquis of Leyde, was a brave man, and his defence of Dunkirk forms one of the most famous episodes in the war. He was only equalled in courage and recklessness by Enghien, who perpetually was in danger of losing his life. At last a portion of the ramparts was destroyed by a mine and a breach éffected. Further resistance was rendered useless. On October 11, 1646, the garrison marched out of Dunkirk with all the honours of war, and Rantzau was made governor. The capture of Dunkirk proved most advantageous to France, for hitherto it had been a nest of pirates who preyed on the French merchantmen. The Dutch did not, however, view Enghien's success with tranquil feelings. The inhabitants of Zealand feared that their commerce would suffer from the competition of Dunkirk, and were not reassured by Mazarin's promise that, during the continuance of the Avar, at any rate, the French government would not be able to think much about trade. The capture of Dunkirk, though it proved to be the first step towards the rupture of the Dutch and French alliance, remains a glorious exploit on the part of Enghien, and reflects immense credit on Mazarin's preparations and diplomacy.

Notwithstanding the check at Orbitello in Italy, the year 1646 was a fortunate one in the history of the minority of Louis XIV. In the Netherlands the Spaniards had lost Courtray, Mardyke, Furnes, and Dunkirk ; in Italy the French had occupied Piombino and Porto Longone. Over Poland, Sweden, and Denmark, French influence was supreme. In spite, however, of the general success of the French arms and diplomacy, the hostility to Mazarin never ceased, and any check to his policy was greeted with joy. All the elements of the Fronde struggle were being rapidly accumulated, and every detail of Mazarin's private life was seized and enlarged upon by his enemies. His avarice and his care for his relations gave opportunities which his opponents were not slow to use, while his foreign origin always rendered his position in France a difficult one.

From 1646 onwards Mazarin definitely began to amass wealth, and to use the advancement of his relations as a means of strengthening his own position in France. In 1647 he forced the Pope Innocent X. to make his brother, Michel Mazarin, a cardinal, and in the same year his nieces and nephews began to arrive in France in order to share the fortunes of their uncle. One of his sisters had married a Martinozzi, and had two daughters ; the other, Signora Mancini, had no less than ten children. In 1647 Anna Maria, the elder of the two Martinozzi children, and one son and two daughters of Signora Mancini, well known later as Laura and Olympia Mancini, arrived at Fontainebleau and were carefully educated. Their arrival was at once made the subject of many satirical Mazarinades which appeared during the years of the Fronde. Each of the three nieces eventually made a brilliant marriage. Anna Maria Martinozzi married the Prince of Conti, brother of Enghien ; while Laura Mancini married Louis of Vendôme, Duke of Merceur, and eldest son of the Duke of Vendôme, and brother of Beaufort ; and Olympia Mancini became Countess of Soissons, and mother of Prince Eugène.

Between 1645 and 1647 Mazarin had to watch every movement of his enemies. Intrigues were the order of the day, but the intriguers found themselves outmatched by the cardinal, whose position was gaining in strength Moreover, he had successfully broken the union between Orleans and Enghien by stirring up the jealousy which was always latent between the families of Orleans and Condé. As the king's uncle and lieutenant-general of France, Orleans held a position of influence. But he was weak and fickle, and Mazarin had great difficulty in keeping him loyal to the true cause. He, however, fully realised that it was only by decisive successes abroad that a satisfactory peace could be secured which would leave his hands free to deal with his enemies at home. Till that peace was made he was forced to play a waiting game, to balance between parties, and to use intrigue and corruption when forcible measures were required. The French armies held the key of the situation, and Mazarin rightly left no stone unturned to win brilliant and decisive victories.

At the end of 1646 the capture of Dunkirk had strengthened the French military position. If a telling blow could be struck at the Spanish power in Italy, it was likely that Spain would realise the futility of further resistance, and would agree to the conditions of peace which Mazarin as minister had seriously put forward through the French representatives early in 1646.

MAZARIN'S CONNECTION WITH THE REBELLIONS IN NAPLES AND ENGLAND

When Mazarin succeeded Richelieu, Italy was still a geographical expression. The Spaniards held the kingdom of the Two Sicilies and the Tuscan ports, and were supreme in the Milanese. The war of Castro between the papacy and a league of princes—a war the outbreak of which had fatally interfered with Richelieu's Italian policy—continued, and was not concluded till 1644. Divided, and lacking all national feeling, Italy was destined to remain a prey to intrigue and open to attack till the pertinacity of the house of Savoy was rewarded, and Italy, in the latter half of the nineteenth century, became a nation.

Mazarin had not been long in office before he determined, in continuance of Richelieu's policy, to hamper the Spaniards by taking advantage of the chronic discontent in Italy, and to attack either the Milanese or the Tuscan ports. At the same time he took every opportunity during the struggle with Spain to stir up the Neapolitans to revolt. Though the gains to France from Mazarin's Italian policy were small, none the less there is something to be said for a policy which hampered Spain for many years and occupied large bodies of her troops.

Spain during the Thirty Years' War had good reason to regret the policy adopted by Charles V. and his successors at Madrid. Instead of attending to the true interests of their country, the Spanish rulers attempted to rule over the Spanish Netherlands and Italy, and involved themselves in all the dynastic schemes of the Austrian Hapsburgs. The interests of the Spanish population were never considered, and the vast Spanish colonies in America were badly managed. Throughout the sixteenth, seventeenth, and eighteenth centuries the national well-being of Spain was subordinated to dynastic considerations. The Peace of the Pyrenees found Spain in a state of decadence, unable to defend the Spanish Netherlands from attack, with her hold on Italy growing weaker each year, and the vision of an Atlantic empire rapidly passing away. Mazarin rightly concentrated his principal attacks upon the Spanish Netherlands.

From that quarter Paris was most easily threatened, and the loss of the Low Countries to Spain would be not only serious to her reputation, but would prove an immense gain to France. As a means to that end the intervention of France in Italy, and the constant attempts of the French fleet to dominate the western basin of the Mediterranean, have a special interest.

In the Milanese, Tuscany, and Naples, Mazarin simply continued the policy of Richelieu, and devoted all his efforts to secure, if not the expulsion from, at any rate the weakening of the hold of the Spaniards upon Italy. But the same influences which checked Richelieu's attempts to carry out his schemes were at work during Mazarin's ministry, and till the end of the Spanish Succession War Italy remained dominated by

Spain. By the formation of a new Italian League, which should include the Pope, Venice, Florence, Parma, and Modena, Mazarin hoped in 1643 to oust the Spaniards from Milan. But as long as the Spaniards held the Tuscan ports the Grand Duke of Tuscany was unwilling to take any action ; and on the death of Urban VIII. his successor, Innocent X., quarrelled with the French cardinal. Nevertheless, though unable to form a league, Mazarin never ceased to stir up opposition to Spain in Milan, in Tuscany, in Naples, and in Sicily. His agents were to be found in many parts of Italy inciting the Italians to throw off the Spanish yoke and to replace it by national governments. Nothing perhaps illustrates better Mazarin's tenacity of purpose and patience than the way in which he allowed no obstacles to check, more than temporarily, the execution of the anti-Spanish policy in Italy which he carried on consistently till 1648. On July 29, 1644, Urban VIII. died, and the Spanish party among the cardinals succeeded in carrying their candidate, the Cardinal Panfilio, who was elected in September as Innocent X. Mazarin was furious. The French envoy Saint-Chamand was replaced by Grémonville, who, it was hoped, would successfully counteract Spanish influence at Rome. The task was a difficult one. Innocent X. repelled the French advances and declared himself in sympathy with the Spanish cause. His actions confirmed his words, and Grémonville was recalled.

Though Mazarin had failed at Rome, he pursued with energy schemes for the overthrow of the Spanish power in Italy, and at once resolved to conquer the Tuscan *presidii* or ports, and then to proceed to the conquest of Naples itself. The Tuscan ports included Orbitello, Porto Ercole, Porto San Stefano, Telamone, Monte Argentaro, Monte Philippo, and Porto Longone in Elba. Before attacking any of these places, Mazarin fixed upon Prince Thomas of Savoy as the French candidate for the Neapolitan throne. The prince came to Paris, and it was agreed that, in the event of his accession to Naples, he should hand over to France Gaëta and another port on the Adriatic. " Mistress of the *presidii* of Tuscany, of Gaëta, and of a port on the Adriatic, and closely allied with the new king of Naples, France would have ruined the Spanish influence in Italy."1

These well-prepared plans were destined to be unsuccessful. The French fleet sailed from Toulon on

April 26, 1646, and Orbitello, with the help of Prince

Thomas, was besieged. On June 14 a Spanish fleet attempted to raise the siege, and a naval battle took place. The Spaniards were defeated, but the Duc de Brézé, the French admiral, was killed. This disaster, coupled with the incapacity of Prince Thomas and the unhealthiness of the coast, proved fatal to the success of the French enterprise.

The siege of Orbitello was raised in July, Prince Thomas abandoned his artillery and returned to Piedmont, and the French fleet retired. Though the French occupied Piombino and Porto Longone, this check to Mazarin's schemes was, as has been pointed out in the last chapter, at once followed by attacks on his policy. His enemies in Paris gladly seized the opportunity of reviling the minister, and Orleans is reported to have said sarcastically, "Voilà de ses entreprises."2 At the same time Henry Condé claimed the post of admiral for his son Enghien, who had married the sister of the Duc de Brézé. Mazarin was, however, equal to the task of resisting the attacks on himself and the claims of the house of Condé. By his advice Anne of Austria reserved to the crown the right of appointing the admiral; while Mazarin, whose check at Orbitello had been compensated for by the capture of Dunkirk on October 11,1646, prepared to carry out the second portion of his Italian scheme, and, while making a fresh attack upon the Tuscan ports, to take advantage of a revolt which had broken out against the Spanish rule in Naples.

During the year 1646 Mazarin had fully realised the necessity for carrying on the war vigorously against Spain. The Dutch, fearful, since the fate of Dunkirk, of a complete French conquest of the Spanish Netherlands, had shown a tendency to ally with Spain. Mazarin consequently made great efforts to draw closer the bonds which united France and Sweden. The latter country, ruled by the eccentric Queen Christina, was still animated by hatred of the Hapsburgs, and the French cardinal had little difficulty in strengthening the alliance between the courts of Paris and Stockholm. Sure of the Swedish alliance, he decided to avenge the check received by the French forces at Orbitello, and, if possible, force Spain to make peace, by again attacking the Spaniards in Italy. The capture of Piombino and Porto Longone had been effected in the autumn of 1646, and while, early in 1647, Enghien (now, on the death of his father in December 1646, the Prince of Condé) proceeded to Lérida, Mazarin found in the Neapolitan revolt an opportunity for still further harassing Spain.

Naples, which the Spanish descendants of Charles V. held, was regarded by them as a valuable treasury. A Neapolitan parliament, indeed, existed, composed of the nobles and people ; but, in spite of repeated promises, the Spanish viceroys rarely, if ever, summoned it. In 1647 the viceroy, the Duke of Arcos, having already taxed most of the necessaries of life, laid a fresh tax upon fruit. A revolt was the immediate result. This revolt was in its early stages no movement for liberty and independence, it was simply directed against the tax on fruit. Under a fisherman called Masaniello the Neapolitans forced the Duke of Arcos to fly to the castle of St. Elmo, while in Palermo an attack was simultaneously made upon the viceroy of Sicily.

Having quieted the people with fair promises, and having compassed the death of Masaniello on July 16, 1647, the Duke of Arcos reimposed the former taxes, and a fresh revolt burst out. This time the rising was directed against the Spanish rule, and was an attempt on the part of the people to secure independence. Like the

Dutch in the preceding century, the insurgents looked abroad for assistance in their struggle against the power of Spain, and by the advice of one Gennaro Annesi they appealed to the Duke of Guise, who was then in Eome. Mazarin was in 1647 not unwilling to seize this opportunity of hampering the Spanish court. "No enterprise," the cardinal wrote, on hearing of Masaniello's rising, " could be more useful to France." He was well aware what the loss of Naples and Sicily would mean to Spain. " The loss of two kingdoms," he said, "would be the mortal blow to that monarchy." But Mazarin's habitual prudence inclined him to act with caution. French expeditions to Italy since the days of Charles VIII. had been conspicuously unsuccessful, and the Neapolitans were proverbially fickle. It was quite likely that the appearance of a French fleet off Naples might lead to a reaction in favour of Spain. At last, after much hesitation, Mazarin proposed to place Condé at the head of a French army which should be sent to Naples. Condé, however, refused. Mazarin had hoped that Condé would be tempted to take part in a Neapolitan expedition in the hope of becoming King of Naples. The motives which prompted Condé's refusal are unknown. His failure at Lérida may have checked his love for distant expeditions ; he may have suspected that Mazarin wished to induce him to accept what was practically banishment.

After Masaniello's death and Condé's refusal to head an expedition to Naples, Mazarin, with justifiable caution, allowed some months to elapse before he took any decided action. In the meantime he collected troops at Piombino and Porto Longone, and he organised, under Francis d'Este, Duke of Modena, with whom an alliance was signed on September 1, 1647, an attack on the Milanese. The conquest of the duchy of Milan would, he expected, rally round France the princes of Mantua, Parma, and Tuscany. As soon as the Neapolitans had definitely broken with Spain and had demanded aid from France, it would be time enough to send them reinforcements. In October the invasion of the Milanese took place, but failed to accomplish anything decisive. Francis d'Este was unfitted to lead an expedition, being irresolute and timid. The Spaniards fortified Cremona, and the Duke of Modena was unable to advance further. As a set-off to this check in North Italy, Mazarin could now hope to win some striking success in Naples. There the perfidy of Don John of Austria, an illegitimate son of Philip IV. and commander of the Spanish fleet, had roused the people to fresh rebellious acts. Having promised to carry out the conditions granted by the viceroy after Masaniello's death, he proceeded to treat Naples as a conquered town. Reprisals followed, and Gennaro Annesi was placed at the head of a republican government which was proclaimed on October 24, 1647. A definite breach had now been made with Spain, and the Neapolitans appealed to France for aid.

Mazarin's anticipations were fulfilled, and, ignoring his previous resolve to make Prince Thomas king, he decided to intervene in Naples with a fleet and an armed force. From this intervention he hoped to be able to place a capable French nominee on the throne of Naples, and to occupy permanently certain strong places on the coast as harbours for the fleet, and as some return to France for the expenses of the expedition. Already, in September, the feather-headend and incapable Duke of Guise had offered his services to the Neapolitans, and in spite of the disapproval of the French government, he sailed to Naples, and on November 15 was received with enthusiasm.

Born in 1614, Guise was brave, generous, but reckless and extravagant. Descended on the female side from the house of Anjou, Guise was anxious to advocate the claims of that house to Naples. Mazarin had little real confidence in the uncertain and rash Duke of Guise, who had by his action forced the hand of the French, government. Reluctantly Mazarin consented to support the duke's candidature, though he had never any confidence in his enterprise. Nevertheless, Mazarin was resolved to wrest Naples from the King of Spain, and in the absence of a better leader it was difficult to refuse the co-operation of a French prince.

Events, however, fully justified Mazarin's forebodings. "The character of the Duke of Guise," he wrote, "gives me pain, fearing that his voyage will hurt and embarrass us from his small experience, when the most discreet politician would be none too skilful." And on November 15 the Duke of Guise was indeed building on very insecure foundations. To obtain any lasting success in Naples it was necessary to seize the forts which commanded the town in order to bring about united action on the part of the nobles and people of Naples, and to induce the Neapolitans to accept a king. "A republic," said Mazarin, " is impracticable, and will only produce divisions of which Spain will take advantage." On December 19 a French fleet arrived, and

Mazarin seems to have resolved at all hazards to expel the Spaniards from Naples. But the arrival of the fleet only intensified the difficulties of the situation. Divisions had already appeared in Naples, and the opposition of the nobles to the populace, to whom Guise was a hero, had increased in intensity. It was when affairs were in this condition that the French fleet, under the Duke of Richelieu, arrived at Naples, and its appearance brought matters to a crisis. No good object could be effected so long as Guise was in Naples. Mazarin declared that the duke's supporters wished to establish a republic on the Dutch model, with Guise as stadtholder. So convinced was the cardinal that the presence of Guise in Naples rendered the execution of his policy impossible, that orders were given for the forcible abduction of the duke. Richelieu, too, was an incapable naval commander, and missed an excellent opportunity of destroying the Spanish fleet. Meanwhile the position in Naples remained unsatisfactory, and divisions and jealousies took the place of any settled policy. As Guise refused to be enticed on any of the ships under Richelieu's command, and continued to pursue his own rash course, the French fleet returned to France, having effected nothing. Deserted by Mazarin, Guise attempted, on

February 12, 1648, but failed to expel by force the Spaniards from Naples. This failure was a serious blow to his popularity; he neglected Gennaro Annesi, and rapidly made himself detested by his cruelties. The King of Spain at once took advantage of the unpopularity of Guise. A new viceroy, the Count d'Oñata, was appointed, who entered into negotiations with Gennaro Annesi, and a plot was arranged for the overthrow of Guise. Convinced that the French duke intended to rule without his aid, Gennaro suddenly, on April 6, 1648, betrayed the city to the Spaniards, and Don John of Austria took possession of the kingdom. Both Naples and Sicily were treated with great severity by the Spaniards, Gennaro was executed, and Guise was imprisoned for many years in Spain.

There never had been any adequate reason for expecting that French intervention would lead to any solid result, and Mazarin, who well knew the Italian character, was wise in hesitating before taking, in 1648, any further important action. Had Guise succeeded in establishing himself, there is little doubt that the cardinal would have supported him, and an expedition was actually being prepared for the spring of 1648. As it was, France had enough on her hands nearer home without seriously weakening herself by distant expeditions on behalf of a fickle and untrustworthy ally. The tax on fruit was not reimposed, and the kingdom of the Two Sicilies returned to its habitual slumbers.

Nor was Mazarin more successful in his relations with the English Royalists. The English Civil War broke out in 1642 and continued till 1648, and during its continuance English influence on the Continent was practically suspended. Though French policy was in no way interfered with by England, the course of the struggle between the Royalists and Parliamentarians was watched with interest in France. Not only was Henrietta Maria a French princess, but the development of republican opinions in England, as in Holland and Naples, was always viewed with apprehension by Mazarin. Occupied at home by the increasing strength of the opposition, and abroad by the exigencies of a great war, Mazarin was unable seriously to consider the question of sending assistance to the cause of Charles I. It was in his opinion an advantage to France that the English nation should be fully occupied at home.

In 1644 Queen Henrietta Maria arrived in Paris. The cause of Charles I. was not flourishing in England,

and Henrietta hoped to procure French assistance. Mazarin, however, showed no eagerness to involve himself in English affairs. Goring, the English ambassador, had associated himself with the Duchess of Chevreuse, and Mazarin naturally feared the intrigues of Henrietta's following. Besides, he had his hands full. France was amply occupied with the struggle with Spain and Austria, and her resources were taxed to the uttermost. In the summer of 1644 Turenne and Condé had defeated the Imperialists in the battle of Freiburg, and the Rhine Valley from Basle to Bacharach was in French hands. The war, however, showed no signs of coming to an end, and all Mazarin's efforts were devoted to crushing his foes. It is doubtful if, under any circumstances, he would have given Henrietta any effectual assistance. He had no wish to see England strong enough to interfere on the Continent, and he seems to have never wavered from his desire to keep England weak. He was therefore willing, in order to perpetuate the divisions in England, to intrigue with the Irish and Scots, and for a time Paris became the centre of the intrigues of English and Irish Roman Catholics. Mazarin, too, was not unwilling that the energy of such adventurers as the landless Duke of Lorraine should be directed to England ; and, encouraged by the Cardinal's suggestion, Henrietta secured from the Duke of Lorraine a promise to bring 10,000 men into England. It only remained to find transport, and the Prince of Orange was asked for the loan of some ships. These plans, however, came to nothing, and in June 1645 the Royalists were decisively beaten at Naseby. Further defeats at Langport and Bristol rendered Charles's cause hopeless, and an agreement between king and parliament seemed a not unlikely event. To Mazarin peace between the two contending parties would in all probability be followed by the restoration of a national unity dangerous to France. The establishment, too, of a military republic was equally to be deprecated and feared. The minister therefore supported the idea of an alliance between King Charles and the Scots, hoping to stir up bitter dissension between them and the parliament. By such an alliance England would remain weak and divided, and unable to oppose the schemes of France on the Continent. To further this policy Montreuil, an able diplomatist, was sent to England, and at once endeavoured to bring about a close alliance between King Charles and the Scots.

All through the year 1646 it seemed that success would crown Mazarin's policy. The parliament could do nothing to prevent the French capture of Dunkirk, while Charles in May placed himself in the hands of the Scots.

Till January 1647, when he was handed over by them to the English Commissioners, a prolongation of the Civil War, and a consequent weakening of England's position with reference to continental politics, was regarded as almost certain. This subtle policy of the cardinal was by no means agreeable to the impatient spirit of Henrietta Maria, who never ceased from her efforts to induce the French court to take active measures on behalf of her husband. Intrigues in Ireland had raised the hopes of the Roman Catholics that the Penal laws would be abolished. Emery, the French controller-general of finance, supported the English queen's projects, and the French clergy offered to subscribe 1,500,000 francs towards the cost of an expedition to be led by the Duke of Bouillon. Though opposed to the establishment of Roman Catholicism, the Scots were by no means opposed to a French alliance. In June 1646 the English parliament heard through their agent in Paris that the agreement between the king and the Scots was the result of Montreuil's mediation, that the queen had received a large sum from the French clergy, and that an Irish army would aid the Scots in bringing about the triumph of the Royalist cause. There is no doubt that the Scottish Presbyterians hated the English Independents, and some of the Scottish leaders were prepared for the outbreak of a fresh eml war ; but the majority of the Scots were mainly anxious for the establishment of Presbyterianism in England, and shrank from acting in close alliance with the French and Irish. Montreuil's mission had in reality failed, and the Presbyterians and Independents were as yet not prepared to settle their differences by recourse to arms.

Events on the Continent rendered it more than liver necessary to intensify the rift between the Scottish and English Presbyterians on the one hand and the Independents on the other. One of Mazarin's pet projects was to compass the annexation of the Spanish Netherlands, and till that project had been carried out it was advisable that England's difficulties at home should be increased. Therefore, in July 1646, a fresh envoy in the person of Belliévre was sent to England to foment dissensions between the Presbyterians and the Independents. Earlier in the month Montreuil had returned from France and had assured Charles of the good intentions of the queen-regent and of Mazarin. Belliévre was sent ostensibly in order to interpose on behalf of Charles, for Henrietta Maria assured the French court that the Scots were about to deliver him to the parliament. Though Mazarin pretended to sympathise with the English queen, he never seems to have regarded the Stuarts as friendly to France. To judge, however, from his words in November 1646, he was ready to aid Charles to the best of his ability. "If the King of Great Britain," he said, " saw with what ardour I continually think of his interests, he would feel great confidence ; for I so sympathise with his miserable lot, that I would willingly shed my own blood to assist him." In counselling Charles to unite closely with the Presbyterians and so to overthrow the Independents and regain his throne, Mazarin was apparently giving sound advice ; in ordering Belliévre not to interfere in the quarrels of parties in England, he was pursuing a statesmanlike course. · But neither he nor Henrietta Maria nor Belliévre ever understood the depth of the religious convictions of either the king or his opponents. Charles, to their astonishment, would not waive his objections to Presbyterianism, and consequently the Scots in January 1647 handed him over to the English Commissioners. The parliament had triumphed, and during 1647 and 1648 Mazarin was fully occupied in bringing the war with the Emperor to a close. He had practically done nothing to aid the Stuarts, but the rise of Cromwell to power brought new.dangers which were averted by statesmanlike measures. As it was, the imprisonment of Charles by the parliament was followed by a period of disorder in England during which Mazarin brought about the Peace of Westphalia.

In spite of this blow to her hopes, Henrietta Maria continued to weave her schemes. It was obvious to her eager mind that so long as the Thirty Years' War continued help from France was not to be looked for. Consequently she bent all her energies in urging Anne of Austria to conclude peace with Austria. But Mazarin held views which ran counter to those of the English queen, and his influence over the queen-mother was incontestable. Still bent on the conquest of the Spanish Netherlands, he had, by persuading the Elector of Bavaria to ratify the Treaty of Ulm, made a distinct step forwards. The success of France in the war against the Hapsburgs was not to be endangered by intervention in English affairs. So long as Charles and the parliament remained mutually hostile, France could persevere in her foreign policy with good hopes of success. In 1688 Louis XIV. in similar circumstances expected equal advantages from the outbreak of civil war in England. But his hopes proved to be baseless, whereas Mazarin's policy proved successful. Not that the French minister was averse to the restoration of Charles. On the contrary, Belliévre worked steadily to effect that object. But the French envoy was unable to understand the firm resolution of the king not to desert the Anglican Church. If Charles would only agree to the proposals of Cromwell and the leading Independents, Belliévre wrote to Mazarin, he might have the English army on his side. But the English king ruined his chances of a restoration partly by his adherence to principle, partly by his failure to convince his opponents of his sincerity. In 1648, when his position had become one of extreme peril both to himself and his supporters, Mazarin was unable even to consider the possibility of weakening the power of the Independent army by sending quite a small reinforcement to the aid of the Scots, who had entered upon the Second Civil War.

In January 1648 the Dutch had made peace with Spain, and Mazarin's hopes of acquiring the Spanish-Netherlands were frustrated. Moreover, when, on October 24, the Peace of AVestphalia was signed, Mazarin found himself involved in a struggle with the

Fronde—a struggle which taxed all his energies, and deprived him of " the power, even if he had the will, to aid in the recovery of Charles's crown."3 No adverse circumstances, however, daunted the brave English queen. Still full of hope, she expected to procure money from Mazarin, and even from Venice, and by these means to make Ireland a strong Royalist centre. Before many months were over her hopes and those of Mazarin were destined to be crushed. Charles died on the scaffold, and Mazarin soon realised that France had to reckon with a powerful military republic which was bent on commercial and colonial expansion.

THE PEACE OF WESTPHALIA

The Peace of Westphalia constitutes an important epoch in the history of Europe. It marked the close of the struggle in Central and Northern Europe between the Reformation and Counter-Reformation movements, and the failure of the attempt of the, Emperor to form all Germany into an Austrian and Roman Catholic empire. After the Peace of Westphalia, commercial rather than religious motives regulated the policy of the chief states of Europe. But the peace did not merely mark a revolution in men's ways of thought; it also signalised a remarkable change in the balance of forces on the Continent. For upwards of a century the Hapsburgs, supreme in Vienna and Madrid, and closely united by family ties, had threatened to impose their will upon

Europe. After 1648 the danger ceased. The weakness of the Emperor and the strength and independence of the German princes rendered any close union with Spain impossible, while Spain herself, though she struggled till 1659 against her impending fate, was already declining power.

From another point of view the Peace of Westphalia has a special interest. It affords an admirable illustration of a successful effort on the part of the German princes to strengthen their own position at the expense of the central power. All over Europe the monarchical principle was being assailed. In Holland the power of the stadtholder depended entirely on the will of the merchant aristocracy ; in England a republic was shortly to be established; in Italy the revolt of Masaniello seemed at one time likely to lead to the formation of a Neapolitan government independent of Spain; and even in Russia aristocratic discontent against the tsar existed. Thus the movement in France against Mazarin, which shortly developed into the Fronde struggle, was but one of many similar manifestations of a general tendency all over Europe to attack monarchical institutions.

Mazarin was well aware of the impossibility of

checking the general disaffection in France till Austria had been humbled, and therefore he devoted all his efforfcs to bringing the war to a successful conclusion. The actual congress was not opened at Münster till April 10, 1644, and it was not till the end of 1645 that the negotiations seriously began. The questions to be settled were many and complicated. France and Sweden demanded compensation either in land or money ; the Elector of Brandenburg wished to occupy all Pomerania which the Swedes had seized ; the Elector Palatine demanded restoration to his dominions. Then there were innumerable questions dealing with the religióus situation, the United Provinces, Italy, Catalonia, Portugal, the constitution of the empire, and the position of the German princes. Early in the proceedings Mazarin brought forward France as the protector tóf the ancient German liberties, and so secured the friendship of the imperial towns and the German princes. The Langrave of Hesse, the Elector of Trêves, the Duke of Neuburg, readily accepted the protection of France. It proved impossible to gain the fickle Duke of Lorraine ; it was equally difficult to win over the powerful Elector of Bavaria. Maximilian I. of Bavaria had played an im-portant part in the Thirty Years' War, but from June

1644 he began to enter into periodical negotiations with Mazarin. The cardinal placed no reliance on these negotiations, which he recognised were meant to sow discord between France and her allies. Consequently it was not till after the battle of Nördlingen, followed later by the devastation of his territory by Turenne, that Maximilian made serious overtures to France. In an atmosphere of intrigue such as existed at Munster, Mazarin did wisely in pressing on military operations.

The capture of Dunkirk in 1646 was rightly regarded as one of the most brilliant exploits of the minority of Louis XIV., and the military reputation of Enghien was greatly increased. But the success which had attended the French arms had serious political consequences. The Dutch became alarmed at the possibility of further conquests on the part of the French, which might result in the practical absorption of the Spanish Netherlands into the French monarchy, and their fears tended to hamper Mazarin's efforts to bring the war to a close. After the fall of Dunkirk that minister thought the way was opened for negotiations with Spain, the most bitter of the enemies of France. Hewas prepared to sacrifice the Catalans and the Portuguese if Spain would relinquish the Spanish Netherlands. As early as January

1646 he had written clearly on this point to the French envoys at Münster, and his letter is a valuable and interesting summary of the views always held by the French nation with regard to the so-called national boundaries of France. Paris would be safe from attack on her north-eastern frontier if the Spanish Netherlands were secured; the possession of Lorraine, Alsace, and Franche Comté would relieve France of all danger from Germany ; and by these acquisitions the power and greatness of the French monarchy would be fully vindicated. In ordinary times opposition from England to the French absorption of the Spanish Netherlands would have taken concrete form, but in 1646 the Civil War was at its height, and England was a *quantité négligeable.* Spain, the cardinal believed, could be easily gained if Catalonia and Portugal were left to her mercies. Mazarin, however, had never calculated upon the strength of the Dutch opposition to his scheme. To satisfy the fears of the merchants of Amsterdam he was prepared to hand over Antwerp to the stadtholder ; and in making this offer he felt that he was adhering to the arrangement for a partition of the Spanish Netherlands, in accordance with the treaty of 1635.But the stadtholder's power was limited, and public opinion in

Holland favoured the opening of direct negotiations with Spain. On hearing that a marriage between the Spanish Infanta and Louis XIV. was being discussed, the Dutch were seized with a justifiable panic, and from the date of the capture of Dunkirk their friendship with France sensibly cooled. This circumstance, coupled with the failure of the Count of Harcourt in November 1646 to take Lerida, presaged further difficulties in the execution of Mazarin's plans in Flanders and Spain. To all appearances, however, the year 1646 had been peculiarly glorious in French history. The Spaniards had lost Courtray, Mardyke, Furnes, and Dunkirk; in Italy the French had occupied Piombino and Porto Longone. France, moreover, was closely allied with Portugal, Catalonia, and Sweden; her influence was preponderant in Poland and Denmark ; and Mazarin had hopes of gaining Bavaria. The Dutch Alliance still existed ; it was by no means impossible that Mazarin's intrigues in England on behalf of the Royalist cause might not bear some fruit, and lead, at any rate, to the prolongation of the Civil War. The success of Mazarin's foreign policy had strengthened his position in Paris, while the death of Senry Bourbon, Prince of Condé, on December 20, 1646, removed one of his most vindictive opponents. His heir and successor, the young Due d'Enghien, was a soldier rather than a politician. To the governments of Champagne and Brie he now, owing to his father's death, added that of Burgundy. At first he did not use his influence against Mazarin. That minister had persuaded the young prince to proceed to Spain and rehabilitate the French fortunes there. The Catalans, afraid of being abandoned by the government of Louis XIV., were on the point of making terms with Spain, and it was hoped in Paris that the young Condé would, in his usual brilliant fashion, win a decisive success and restore confidence to the French allies.

During Condé's absence in Spain important events took place in Germany. In the autumn of 1646 Turenne had effected a junction with Wrangel, who, on the illness of Torstenson, had succeeded to the command of the Swedish troops. Together they invaded and devastated Bavaria, and in December the Duke Maximilian had solicited a suspension of arms. In March 1647 the Treaty of Ulm was signed, and Austria was deprived of the valuable Bavarian alliance. The duke's lands were secured from all further devastation, and a distinct step was taken towards the conclusion of the war. For Mazarin this Treaty of Ulm came at an opportune time.

The Dutch had just made a truce with Spain, though their defection was as yet limited to a suspension of hostilities, and their co-operation in the Spanish Netherlands could no longer be counted upon. Owing, however, to the Treaty of Ulm, Mazarin was now able to transfer to Flanders many of the troops then serving in Germany. Turenne, indeed, wished to unite with the Swedes, to march to Vienna, and so to force the Emperor to make peace. As events turned out this project might have been carried out with advantage. But at the time of the Treaty of Ulm the Emperor was showing a more conciliatory temper, while the Spaniards, overjoyed by the defection of the Dutch from the French cause, constituted a serious danger to France.

Mazarin was, therefore, justified in deciding to concentrate his principal efforts in the Spanish Netherlands. There, under the Archduke Leopold, the army of Spain took Armentieres (June 4, 1647) and Landrecies (July 28). The capture of Dixmude (July 13) and La Bassée (July 29) by Rantzau and Gassion relieved the situation, and Mazarin resolved to attempt the complete conquest of the Spanish Netherlands, and looked to Turenne to carry out this plan. Unfortunately the Weimarian troops who were serving under Turenne mutinied, and all Mazarin's schemes were frustrated. This proved to be the beginning of a series of disasters to France which encouraged her enemies and seemed to render all hope of peace impossible. The Duke of Bavaria began to show a disposition to throw over his arrangements with France, and in Bohemia the Swedish army in August suffered a severe repulse. In Spain, Condé failed to take Lérida, and on June 17, 1647, raised the siege. In Naples the situation was by no means encouraging, and Mazarin wisely refrained from undertaking any serious enterprise on behalf of so fickle a people as the Neapolitans. In England the Parliamentary party were victorious and all chance of Royalist successes was at an end.

At the beginning of October, however, the position of France in Europe seemed to be more hopeful, and Mazarin's power more firmly established. Supreme at court, he had with him in France relations by whose marriages he hoped still further to strengthen his position. The French armies were superior to those of the enemy in Germany, Flanders, and Italy. France held possession of Piombino, Porto Longone, Pinerolo, Cásale, Philipsburg, Dunkirk, Alsace, and Lorraine. Though checked at Lerida, she had not lost her hold on

Catalonia. Holland's defection had not yet led to active opposition, and the Treaty of Ulm indicated the approach of peace. Had it not been for the unfortunate mutiny of the Weimarian troops, signal successes would probably have been gained in Flanders by Turenne. Even in Naples the prospects of French intervention looked hopeful, and at the end of the month the Neapolitans proclaimed a Republic. At home Mazarin's power and influence seemed assured. Emery had been made *contrôleur-général* and admitted into the royal Council, and Mazarin appeared to hold the reins of office as firmly as did Richelieu. It was about this time that he opened his famous library and introduced the opera into France. In 1647 *Orpheus and Eurydice* was performed. Following in the footsteps of Richelieu, Mazarin began to patronise literature. Among those who received pensions were Corneille, Balzac, Chapelain, Voiture, and Descartes.

From the beginning of October 1647, however, these appearances of strength, prosperity, and good-fortune were seen to be ephemeral, and till the end of the year misfortune dogged Mazarin's footsteps. Gassion and Rantzau failed to win any decisive success in Flanders, and Gassion was himself killed on October 5.

In the Milanese the French operations proved futile, and in Naples the folly of the Duke of Guise had by the end of the year ruined all chance of effective intervention on the part of France in Naples. The cardinal was justified in believing that the year 1647 had been under the influence of an evil constellation. Nor did the opening of 1648 give any indication of decisive French successes. In January the Dutch made a definitive treaty with Spain, while the Elector of Bavaria, who in October 1647 had taken up arms again, renounced the Treaty of Ulm.

The situation at the beginning of 1648 was thus far from being encouraging. Mazarin, however, never lost hope or relaxed his efforts. The failure of Condé at Lerida had been followed by the issue of a vast number of satirical attacks upon him, and the cardinal, Paul de Condi, the poet Sarrasin, the Comte de Fiesque, and the Bishop of Rennes were especially conspicuous in the virulence of this hostility to the government. Nor was the *parlement* of Paris idle ; it seized the opportunity of testifying its opposition to the minister. Energetic measures were at once taken to relieve the situation. To Condé was given the command of the army in Flanders, vacant by the death of Gassion, while Turenne was ordered to attack the Duke of Bavaria, and the Marshals

Plessis-Praslin and Schömberg were entrusted with operations in Italy and Spain.

In May the combined Franco-Swedish forces under Turenne and Wrangel won the battle of Zusmarshausen, and Bavaria was invaded. At the same time another Swedish general, Königsmark, entered Bohemia and threatened Prague. The Emperor was thus attacked both from the west and from the north. In Paris, which was seething with sedition, the victory of Zusmarshausen was little noticed, though Mazarin fully appreciated its importance, and had little doubt that the Emperor would be compelled to make peace. · But before this desired end was attained he had to live through many anxious months. In Italy the operations were disappointing. Plessis-Praslin won no decisive success in the Milanese, and no satisfactory opportunity for successful intervention in Naples presented itself. Nor were the first beginnings of Condé's campaign in Flanders promising. Courtray was lost in May, and it was expected in Holland that the French would not be able to keep possession of their conquests.

In July, however, the tide turned. On the 13th of that month Schomberg captured Tortosa, and Spain lay open to a French advance. On the 26th a still more important success was gained, which brought into clear relief the value of the victory of Zusmarshausen. Königsmark, the Swedish general, cleverly seized Little Prague, that portion of Prague which was situated on the left bank of the Moldau. It was the capture of Little Prague which perhaps more than any other event induced the Emperor to listen to the advice of the Duke of Bavaria and of other German princes, and to agree to peace. Hardly had Mazarin heard the news of these successes when the Duke of Châtillon arrived with the welcome intelligence of Condé's defeat of the Spaniards on August 22 at Lens.

Rarely has a victory been won at a more opportune moment, and the debt due to Condé by the French government was immense. The French had, earlier in the year, lost Courtray, and had failed to take Ostend, and the Archduke Leopold, a commander of ability, had pressed forward to the line of the Somme. Condé, at the head of a very inferior force, lacking supplies, pay, and ammunition, was opposed to him, and on his success much depended. Paris was in a state bordering on revolution, the treasury was bankrupt, the provinces threatened to rise, and the court, opposed by the *parlement,* many of the nobles, and the populace, was distracted. Madame de Chevreuse, Beaufort, and others of the *Important* faction had again appeared, and even treasonable communications with Spain were hinted at. The attitude of Paris in many respects foreshadowed that taken up in 1789. At Lens on August 20 Condé met the Spanish army, which occupied a strong position. Fortunately Leopold, confident of victory, advanced into the plain, where he was attacked by the French. After a desperate struggle, in which fortune inclined first to one side and then to the other, Condé, having shown military qualities of the highest order, won a decisive and splendid victory. The news of the victory of Lens revived the hopes of Mazarin and the courage of the affrighted court, France was saved from invasion, and the supporters of the French monarchy took fresh heart. " At last," said Mazarin, " Heaven has declared in our favour." From this succession of victories he was justified in anticipating important results. The Spaniards, he declared, would become more tractable on the question of peace, and he fully expected that the French court would be enabled to triumph over the *parlement* of Paris. Though on both these points Mazarin was destined to be disappointed, the Peace of Westphalia was an immediate and striking result of the French and Swedish successes in Germany.

From this peace the Spaniards held aloof. Servien, Mazarin's able minister at Münster, had fully realised that, since the conclusion of the treaty with Holland in January 1648, Spain had no intention of coming to terms with France. In Madrid much was hoped for from the troubles in France, full reports of which were furnished by the Duchess of Chevreuse and Saint-Ibal. Moreover, the Spaniards were confident in the superiority of their armies. They had reconquered Naples, and Plessis-Praslin in October was compelled to raise the siege of Cremona. Their defeat at Lens was in their eyes fully compensated for by the sedition in Paris and the condition of the French armies. In a word, Spain in October 1648 considered herself fully competent to vanquish France.

The Emperor was in a very different position. The victory of the French at Zusmarshausen, and that of the Swedes at Prague, placed his capital at the mercy of his enemies, who were preparing to cross the Inn and invade his hereditary dominions. Mazarin, hampered by the progress of the Fronde, and anxious to have his hands free, showed a conciliatory spirit, and the Emperor, in opposition to the strongly-expressed wishes of his Spanish allies, agreed to the French terms.

On October 24, 1648, the Peace of Westphalia was signed between France and Sweden on the one hand, and the representatives of the Emperor and the Empire on the other. France secured Upper and Lower Alsace, the Sundgau, and the prefecture of ten imperial towns ; in other words, the practical ownership of Alsace, though the rights of the imperial princes were for a long time a matter of difficulty. She also obtained recognition of her possession of (1) Metz, Toul, and Verdun, the three bishoprics conquered by Henry III., with their districts, (2) of Old Brisach, situated on the right bank of the Rhine; while the privilege of keeping a garrison in Philipsburg was also granted to France. Further, no fortress was to be placed on the right bank of the Ehine between Basle and Philipsburg. Indirectly France gained enormously. Her ally, Sweden, secured a foothold in Northern Germany, together with a vote in the Diet; and the practical independence of the princes of the Empire was recognised.

Mazarin had successfully carried on the foreign

policy of Richelieu, and the situation of the great European States in 1648 speaks volumes for his skill and energy. The power of the house of Hapsburg was in many respects seriously curtailed. The Austrian branch could no longer aim at establishing a universal monarchy, and came out of the war with its resources much weakened. The Spanish branch had lost its preponderance in Italy, Portugal had regained its independence, Catalonia was in revolt. Though Spain continued the war till 1659, she only lost by doing so, and her defeats and losses strengthened the position of France. French influence remained supreme in Germany for some thirty years, and was only destroyed by the ambition and short-sightedness of Louis XIV. Mazarin had not merely advanced the boundary of France towards the Rhine ; he had established French preponderance in Europe, and had insisted on the recognition of the balance of power. The Peace of the Pyrenees in 1659 completed the work of the pacification of Westphalia. The conclusion of the war between France and the Emperor was hardly noticed in Paris, and this fact in itself is a striking illustration of the want of patriotism of the Frondeurs. Moreover, de Retz, in October 1648, was actually considering the advisability of inviting the Spaniards to march on Paris. His plan was to send Saint-Ibal, his friend and relation, to Brussels to engage Fuensaldaña to advance. Already the Parliamentary Fronde was falling into the hands of plotters and traitors.

THE PARLIAMENTARY FRONDE

There is no doubt that the continuation of the war had completely disorganised the financial administration. Various devices such as the *toisé* had been employed by the government to raise funds, but each attempt had been met by fresh opposition. In 1647 recourse was had to a tax known as the *édit du tarif,* which modified the existing regulations upon the entry of provisions into Paris. Great opposition was raised by the *parlement,* which still more violently opposed in January 1648 a tax upon all possessors of lands. A *lit de justice* was necessary to provide for the requirements of the government.

The operation of the unpopular tax, or *rachat,* as it was termed, was postponed, and the creation of many new *maîtres de requêtes* provided a certain amount of money. At the *lit de justice,* Omer Talon, the intrepid *avocat - général,* delivered an eloquent oration on the condition of the French peasants. " For ten years, Sire," he said, "the country has been ruined, the peasants reduced to sleep upon straw, their furniture sold to pay taxes. To minister to the luxury of Paris millions of innocent people are obliged to live upon rye and oat bread, and their only protection is their poverty." The creation of new *maîtres de requêtes* was stoutly opposed, but in vain, Broussel distinguishing himself by his attacks upon the government.

Thus, while victory was being prepared by Turenne, Condé, and Schomberg, a revolution was breaking out in Paris, and in many other parts of the kingdom resistance to the government was the order of the day. Brittany and Toulouse showed especial audacity in their attacks on government officials. At his wits' end for money, Emery resolved to demand as a condition of the renewal of the *paulette* (a tax paid by those officials whose offices were hereditary) a fine of four years' salary. In the hope of conciliating the *parlement* of Paris, the fine was not imposed on that body. The *parlement,* however, placed itself at the head of the opposition, and on May 13, 1648, it and the Sovereign Courts (the *Chambre des Comptes,* the *Cour des Aides,* and the *Grand Conseil)* signed a bond of union, and the courts decided to send representatives to a conference in the Chamber of St. Louis. Like Louis XVI. in 1789, the queen-mother endeavoured to prevent the meeting of the deputies. Like Louis she failed in her object, and the court was forced to yield. The Spaniards had taken Oourtray, and it was well to temporise. Money was urgently needed, and Mazarin hoped, by appealing to the patriotism of the *parlement,* to obtain the requisite supplies. He represented that the conduct of the *parlement* strengthened the cause of Spain, and ruined the credit of France. Unless money was forthcoming it would be impossible to keep up the French armies, or to maintain order at home. Catalonia would have to be abandoned, the alliance with Sweden and Hesse would be broken off ; in a word, all would be lost. The *parlement,* however, was dead to all sense of patriotism, and was prepared to sacrifice the nation to its own petty interests. Orleans, who had joined the malcontents, promised that the deputies who had been imprisoned or exiled by Mazarin should be restored. Mazarin, hoping for some striking success on the frontier, determined to temporise, and on June 30, 1648, in open defiance of the orders of the government, the Chamber of St. Louis was constituted as a permanent political body to carry out reforms. With its establishment the First or Parliamentary Fronde began its stormy career.

In appearance the *parlement* of Paris was like the English parliament, bent on securing valuable constitutional rights. Its members demanded proper control of the taxes, liberty for the individual, the abolition of *lettres de cachet.* But in doing so they were encroaching upon the rights of the States-General, which was the only representative assembly of the French nation. And, moreover, it was soon evident that the *parlement* aimed primarily at securing its own privileges. Each step in the struggle between the *parlement* and the crown brings out more conclusively the selfishness of the lawyers and their lack of statesmanship. In the New or Second Fronde the nobles made no pretence of securing for the nation constitutional rights. They openly demanded provincial governments, pensions, and gifts of money. Thus the principal cause of the failure of the Fronde movement was apparent from the first. The *parlement* had no constitutional basis ; its opposition to Mazarin, which was in many respects justified, was tainted by the egoism and selfishness of its members. It had in reality no great aims ; it had no hold on the people. As time went on the movement was rapidly wrecked by the intervention of the nobles and court ladies. De Retz was under the influence of the Duchess of Chevreuse ; the Duke of Beaufort was governed by the Duchess of Montbazon ; Condé revealed all his plans to the Duchess of Châtillon, who conveyed them to Mazarin ; Turenne was encouraged in disloyalty by the Duchess of Longueville. There was no lack of ability on the side of the opposition; Molé and de Retz represented talents of different qualities, and the latter remained the most brilliant pamphleteer of the period. Rochefoucauld, who at one time was under the sway of the Duchess of Longueville, gives ample evidence in his *Maximes* of consummate ability and of a profound knowledge of human nature ; while Turenne and Condé, who at the period were united against the crown, were the two ablest generals of the day. Among other conspicuous men of the day who opposed Mazarin, Chavigny and Châteauneuf were perhaps the most dangerous.   But the association of most of these heroes of the Fronde with the court ladies ruined all chance of success. Love affairs and politics became hopelessly intermingled, and the New Fronde has remained a ridiculous episode in French history. Though the Old Fronde was narrow-minded and selfish, and the New Fronde absurd, the movements were fraught with great danger to the monarchy. In 1648 Mazarin at first failed to recognise the gravity of the situation, and he thought that he had only to combat the intrigues of some of the nobles. In the later phases of the struggle he often erred through his belief in diplomacy and his tendency to follow moderate counsels. But he never faltered in his determination to preserve the rights of the French monarchy ; he easily outmatched his oppo-nents in intrigue ; and eventually, supported by the *bourgeoisie* and the mass of the nation, he triumphed over both the *parlement* and the nobles.

Throughout the early months of 1648 the opposition of the *parlement* was intensified by the folly and unpopularity of Emery, the superintendent of the finances, and by the failure of Mazarin to master the details of the French administrative system. Moreover, he had given some justification for the attacks made upon him by the favours which he showered upon his own relations, and by the means employed in order to secure for his brother the title of cardinal. The truth is, Mazarin cared little for home affairs, and gave no thought to matters connected with the commerce and agriculture of France. Unlike Henry IV. and Richelieu, he made no attempt to open up new sources of prosperity for France, by founding colonies, encouraging trade, introducing manufactures, or protecting agriculture.

His neglect of the internal administration was largely answerable for the financial embarrassments of France, for the misery of the people, and to a large extent for the outbreak of the First Fronde. At the same time it must be remembered that his predecessor was in some measure responsible for the troubles which ensued after his death. Richelieu had made no efforts to reform the financial administration of France, and both the direct and indirect taxes were levied unfairly and oppressively. The financiers who farmed the indirect taxes made enormous fortunes out of the taxpayers ; fraud and peculation were common ; the provinces were in a state of wretchedness. The sale of ónices, the system of farming the taxes, and the *gabelle* or tax on salt were left untouched ; the enormous and harmful concessions given to the nobles during the minority of Louis XIII. had not been revoked or diminished. On his accession to office, Mazarin found that the revenues of the next three years had been spent. Moreover, on Richelieu's death few men of marked capacity were to be found in France. Like Frederick the Great in the next century, Richelieu was jealous of any initiative, on the part of his colleagues. He gradually concentrated in his own hands all the threads óf the administration, and controlled the generals in the field. His system produced useful agents, but neither statesmen nor able commanders. The concentration of all authority in his own hands checked reforms in the government departments, and one writer has stated that " the Fronde would never have taken place if Richelieu had thought more of securing efficiency in those departments to which he could not give sufficient personal attention, and less on concentrating all authority in his own hands."

After Richelieu's death a policy of firmness, if not severity, was required. The easy rule of Anne of Austria, with its pardons and concessions, resulted in an increase of independence on the part of the nobles, and led ultimately to the Fronde. The policy of leniency brought numerous difficulties and dangers which Mazarin in the end succeeded in overcoming. That he was able to do so was probably due partly to his own perseverance, partly to the policy of Richelieu, who had weakened the nobles and the *parlement* and deprived them of all substantial power. Had Richelieu lived the Fronde could never have occurred ; that it did occur "was due to Mazarin's inability to rule with the same iron hand as his more illustrious predecessor."

Rarely has a minister, occupied in carrying on a prolonged war, been so involved in internal difficulties as was Mazarin. He had to superintend the movements of French generals in Flanders, Germany, Italy, and Spain, and at the same time to keep in constant communication with his agents at Münster, who carried on complicated peace negotiations under his instructions.

During the earlier years of his ministry, successes abroad strengthened the government at home and enabled it to take up a firm attitude towards its opponents. In 1643 the victory of Rocroi had aided in the establishment of Anne of Austria's regency ; in 1645 the triumph at Nördlingen had enabled Mazarin to suppress the rising opposition of the *parlement* of Paris ; and in 1646 the capture of Mardyke, Dunkirk, Piombino, and Porto Longone had effaced the recollection of the failure at Orbitello. But in 1648 the situation at home was more critical, and political passions ran high. Mazarin's neglect of the internal administration had led to the revival of the cabals suppressed in 1643, while *the parlement* of Paris found in the general misery and misgovernment of the country some justification for its opposition to the court and the minister. Turenne's victory of Zusmarshausen in May 1648 passed almost unnoticed in Paris, which was then seething with discontent. Mazarin, however, hoped that a victory won by the popular Condé in Flanders would at any rate arrest attention, strike the imagination of the Parisians, and enable the court to deal a telling blow at its opponents.

That the opposition had any real ground of complaint Mazarin never seems to have acknowledged, and he certainly at this time failed to grasp the gravity of the situation. The leaders of the Parliamentary Fronde were to a great extent men who "represented the highest type of citizen life," and who had the welfare of France at heart. In attacking a wasteful administration and a ruinous system of taxation, the Fronde movement is deserving of respect. There was much to urge against the frauds of contractors, unjust imprisonments, and the creation of new offices, and many of the suggested reforms of the Chamber of St. Louis were excellent. On May 15, 1648, delegates from the four Sovereign Courts, viz. the *Parlement,* the *Grand Conseil,* the *Chambre des Comptes,* the *Cour des Aides,* had met in the Chamber of St. Louis, "to reform the abuses which had crept into the State." The thirty-two delegates who sat in that Chamber formulated their demands, and practically claimed a share in the legislative authority. Their principal demands were—

That no tax should be levied unless previously voted by the *parlement* of Paris.

That no one should be kept in prison for more than twenty-four hours without being tried.

That an investigation into the extortions of the farmers of the taxes should be made.

That a quarter of the *taille* should be remitted, and that money gained from that source should be strictly appropriated to the wars.

That the intendants should be abolished.

That no new office should be created without the agreement of the *parlement* of Paris.

The *parlement* of Paris thus proposed to take up a position similar to that occupied by the English parliament. But the *parlement* of Paris was unfitted to be a legislative body. It was merely a close corporation of hereditary lawyers, whose claim to political functions had been summarily dismissed by Richelieu. The demand for the abolition of the intendants at once testifies to its want of statesmanship.

Among Richelieu's beneficial measures none was more valuable than the appointment of the intendants. By abolishing them the *parlement* of Paris was threatening the unity of the whole internal administration. Without the intendants the provinces would once again fall into the incapable hands of the nobles, feudalism would again be rampant, and general confusion and anarchy would ensue. The *parlement* no doubt attacked the intendants in the hope of succeeding to their functions and thus securing a considerable voice in the administration of the provinces. The intendants, too, whose full title was *intendants of justice, police, and finance,* had often infringed upon the jurisdiction of the *parlement,* which was always jealous of any invasion of its judicial powers. The proposals of the Chamber of St. Louis constituted a distinct attack on the royal power; they also implied on the part of the Sovereign Courts an invasion of the rights of the nation. The king alone had legislative power, and the States-General alone had the right to present to him their grievances. At this crisis it is evident that the *parlement* wished to supersede the States-General and to take their place. Such a usurpation on the part of a body of lawyers could not be tolerated either by the government or by the nation, and the resistance of the former eventually received the full support of the French people.

Anne of Austria, in her determination to preserve for her son all the royal prerogatives intact, was furious at the demands of the Sovereign Courts, and was prepared to enter upon a contest with them without delays Mazarin, however, persuaded her to temporise. Orleans in July 7 presided over a conference in his palace, and certain concessions were made by Mazarin to the opposition. The superintendent Emery was dismissed, and the incapable Marshal de la Meilleraye substituted. A chamber of justice was set up, to deal with all abuses connected with the financial administration.

Over the abolition of the intendants there was much angry discussion. Eventually Anne gave a reluctant consent to the suppression of all except those in Languedoc, Provence, the Lyonnais, Picardy, and Champagne. During these conferences Orleans showed a sympathy with the Frondeurs, and it was evident that he would not uphold the royal cause. Being determined at the first opportunity to resist the pretensions of the *parlement,* and being desirous to sound the loyalty of Condé, Anne and Mazarin summoned the prince to Paris. It was probably arranged at some interviews which took place on July 19 and the following day that the prince should first crush the Archduke Leopold and then return to aid the government in overcoming the resistance of the *parlement.*

Till Condé had won a decisive victory the government thought it well to continue to temporise, and Anne of Austria simulated a desire to satisfy all the demands of the Frondeurs. On July 31 a royal declaration agreed to the majority of the claims made by the Sovereign Courts in the Chamber of St. Louis. No satisfactory guarantee was, however, given with regard to the personal liberty of the subject, and Broussel and other extremists continued to agitate. The situation, which in many respects resembled that of 1792, remained critical, the Frondeurs desiring further radical changes, while the court anxiously awaited developments on the frontier. At last, on August 22, 1648, arrived the news of Condé's victory at Lens.

"Heaven has at last declared in our favour," wrote Mazarin, "in the Low Countries no less than in other places." The victories of Zusmarshausen, Tortosa, and Prague had now been crowned by the victory of Lens. The superiority of the French arms was proved, and the court prepared to crush the opposition of the *parlement.* The success at Lens would in Mazarin's opinion enable him to force Spain to make peace, and to triumph over the *parlement.*   By the advice of the Count of Chavigny, the King's Council—which included, besides the queen-regent and Mazarin, the Dukes of Orleans and Longueville, the Chancellor Seguier, and Meilleraye, the superintendent of the finances—decided, like the court of Louis XVI. in July 1789, to carry out a *coup d'état* and to arrest three members of the *parlement,* Broussel, Blancmesnil, and Charton. The arrests were to take effect in August. On August 26, the day on which a *Te Deum* was being sung in Notre Dame in honour of the victory at Lens, the attempt to carry out the *coup d'état* was made. Unlike Charles I. in his attempt to arrest the five members, the action of the French government was partially successful. Charton indeed escaped, but Broussel and Blancmesnil were seized. The populace of Paris at once rose, and erected barricades. The whole city was in an uproar. The news that Masaniello had headed a rising in Naples against the tax-gatherers helped to excite the mob, just as the victories of the English parliament had encouraged the aspirations of the French *parlement.* At this point Paul de Gondi, better known as the Cardinal de Retz, the intriguing coadjutor of the Archbishop of Paris, became prominent. He appeared at the Palais-Royal and advised the queen-regent to yield to the popular wish and release Broussel and Blancmesnil. Having failed in his object, he set to work to inflame still more the passions of the multitude. On August 27 the situation became yet more serious, and the Chancellor Seguier, attacked by the mob, nearly lost his life.

The *parlement* endeavoured, at first without success, to induce Anne to release the prisoners ; but at length, yielding to the advice of Orleans and Mazarin, she consented to a compromise. The *parlement* agreed not to interfere in political matters, and Broussel and

Blancmesnil were released. The barricades disappeared, and outwardly Paris was pacified.

But all danger was by no means over. The Duke of Longueville had during the troubles held a very ambiguous attitude, and it was evident that he and other nobles were not loyal to the court. The troops had shown signs of mutiny; the days of the League seemed likely to return. On August 29 Mazarin made certain suggestions to the regent which testified to his foresight and determination. He was resolved to restore the royal authority, and to subdue the *parlement.* He was determined to enforce the supremacy of the king in Paris, and till that had been accomplished the reputation of France would suffer abroad, trade would languish, Jbhe conclusion of the war would be deferred. Like Mirabeau, Mazarin recognised the necessity of removing the king and court from the influence of the capital. He therefore advised the departure of the court to Rueil, Conflans, or Saint Maur, where the return of Condé could be awaited. On that general's arrival Paris could, if necessary, be coerced by force of arms. Meanwhile he urged the adoption of temporising measures, and of a policy of conciliation, with the object of dividing the enemies of the royal authority. Many of the *bourgeoisie* were opposed to the late seditious conduct of Paris, and the older members of the *parlement* were disposed to peace. But a powerful party in the *parlement* was determined to regain its political powers, and on the instigation of de Retz held meetings in order to consult upon the necessary measures to be taken. Moreover, the Count of Chavigny had deserted the cause of the court and urged the *parlement* to resist Mazarin to the uttermost. It was obvious that a further collision between the royal authority and thé *parlement* was inevitable.

Mazarin's mind was made up. On September 13 the court moved to Rueil, where it was joined by Orleans, Seguier, Meilleraye, and Condé. Two of the cardinal's opponents, the Marquis of Châteauneuf and the Count of Chavigny, at once felt the heavy hand of the minister. The former was exiled; the latter was placed under arrest. The attempt of a deputation of the *parlement,* headed by its president, Matthieu Molé, to secure the release of Chavigny and to induce the queen-regent to return to Paris, failed, and the King's Council annulled the decree of the *parlement* itself. The *parlement* prepared to take defensive measures, but the outbreak of hostilities was averted by the temporary triumph of a pacific spirit in the court. It is difficult to account for this sudden change; it was probably due to the fact that Mazarin could not depend upon the whole-hearted support of Condé in carrying out an energetic policy. Condé indeed stood apart from de Retz and looked with contempt upon the "long-robed" *parlement* as much as he did upon the *canaille.* Like Napoleon he scorned mob-rule and disorder. But for years he had been alienated from Mazarin, and hated him as much as he despised the Frondeurs.

Yielding to the persuasions of de Retz, Condé advocated the assembling of a conference, hoping to bring about Mazarin's exclusion from its meetings. The conference first met at Saint-Germain on September 25, the royal authority being represented by Orleans, Condé, Conti, and Longueville ; and it lasted ten days, till October 4. After long discussions, the members agreed to an ordinance, which was published on October 22, 1648, and known as the Declaration of Saint-Germain. Most of the demands of the Chamber of St. Louis were conceded. The financial, judicial, and commercial administration of the kingdom was regulated, and measures were taken to check arbitrary arrests and to reform the methods of taxation. This ordinance was the most important act of the First or Parliamentary Fronde, and represents the high-water mark of constitutional advance made by the *parlement* and its supporters. It almost seemed that constitutional life was at last to begin in France. But if examined closely the Declaration of October 22 bears full evidence as to the selfish and narrow aims of the *parlement,* and shows how every so-called constitutional effort on its part was tainted by its determination to secure its own privileges. In the Declaration it is specially stated that the charges and privileges of the *parlement* should be guaranteed. Though the regular payment of the *rentes* of the Hôtel de Ville—a matter in which the *bourgeoisie* was interested—was enforced, and though there was a reference in general terms to the amelioration of the lot of the mass of the people, the Declaration was principally concerned with securing and confirming the privileges of the *parlement.*

So far Mazarin and Anne had been forced to yield, and the *parlement* had apparently won the day. But Mazarin had only simulated a yielding spirit ; in reality he was more determined than ever to establish the royal authority, to crush all opposition in Paris by a concentration of troops under a trusted commander. By his advice Anne had made promises which she never intended to keep, and Mazarin was simply biding his time. One of his most striking characteristics was his perseverance in carrying out his plans. Having fixed upon a policy, he carried it through in the end, though compelled to adopt various and unexpected methods before success was attained. It is noteworthy that the Treaty of Westphalia and the treaty with the Frondeurs was signed on the same day. It is equally noteworthy that, while the Frondeurs were seemingly triumphant, Mazarin was making careful preparations for the civil war which he regarded as inevitable.

On October 30 the court returned to Paris, and two months of anxiety followed. Orleans was with difficulty induced to forgo his feelings of resentment towards Mazarin, and to remain faithful to the royal cause. His support was all the more valuable as the *parlement* was disposed to harass the government at every opportunity. It complained that the promises in the Declaration of October 22 were not carried out, that the grievances of the taxpayers had not been remedied; moreover, like the National Assembly in 1789, it was much agitated at the gradual concentration of troops round Paris. Though Orleans and Condé visited the *parlement* in December and promised that the Declaration of October 22 should be loyally executed, the attacks on the government, and especially on Mazarin, increased in violence. Countless pamphlets styled Mazarinades were published containing abuse of the cardinal. " It was the fashion to hate Mazarin," is the declaration of a court lady, and the hatred was shared by the nobles and the workmen of Paris. He gained no thanks for the conclusion of the Peace of Westphalia, but was attacked for not bringing the war with Spain to a close. These attacks on the cardinal were intensified by the support which they gained from de Retz. In the existing complications lay his chance of securing at least notoriety. Utterly unprincipled, and absolutely devoid *of* any patriotic feelings, de Retz hoped during the coming troubles to become the practical ruler of Paris. For five years Paris read little else but Mazarinades, which, with very rare exceptions, were utterly devoid of literary merit. These attacks on his authority and position implied, in Mazarin's opinion, the growth of revolutionary views, and he warned the queen-mother that the situation in France resembled that in England at the opening of the Civil War. He thought that his own position was like Strafford's, and he was prepared to act vigorously. The encroachments on the royal power increased, and the cardinal advocated a fresh retirement from Paris. On January 5, 1649, the court, under circumstances of haste and secrecy, moved suddenly to Saint-Germain, and the Parisians the following morning "saw war, siege, and famine at their gates." The Civil War had "Begun, and continued from January 6 to April 1, 1649. Mazarin hoped, by means of the troops, to cut Paris off from all supplies and to starve it into surrender. But the army of 15,000 was not large enough for carrying out so elaborate a scheme, and Mazarin had to be content with occupying the principal posts outside the city. Under Condé the military operations were efficiently performed, and the Parisians, with their hastily-raised army, could do little but defend themselves. Though risings took place in the north and south-east, the war of the First Fronde concentrated itself round the capital. At first Paris adopted a bold attitude. Under the influence of the Duchess of Longue-ville, who now " sank to the level of a mere adventuress," the Frondeurs were joined by many princes, such as her brother the Prince of Conti, her husband the Duke of Longueville, the Marshal de la Mothe, the Duke of Bouillon, and the Duke of Beaufort. The latter together with de Retz became the real leaders of the resistance to the court, and were the last to be reconciled to the government. While de Retz headed the parliamentary movement, Beaufort, " the idol of the markets," led the mob. Hoping to stir up the provinces, the Duke of Longueville proceeded to Normandy; but Mazarin at once sent the Count of Harcourt to suppress all rebellious movements. In spite of this danger, and of small risings in the south-west, the war of the First Fronde was mainly an attempt on the part of the *parlement* of Paris to remedy certain existing evils in the government, though de Retz hoped to win a decisive success by means of the treason of Turenne.

The treason of Turenne was more serious than possible rebellions in the provinces. That general, perhaps beguiled by the Duchess of Longueville, proposed to lead his army, composed mainly of Germans, to Paris. Fortunately the German auxiliaries refused to follow him, and Turenne was compelled later to retire to Heilbronn, and thence to Holland.

Freed from all fear of any serious risings in the provinces, and for the moment from any hostile movement

on the part of Turenne, Mazarin was able to devote his energies to the task of subduing Paris. There, on

January 12, the mob had seized the Arsenal, and had secured possession of the Bastille. Two days later, on January 14, Beaufort occupied Charenton, important as facilitating the entry of provisions into Paris. Possessed of Charenton and of the town of Brie-Comte-Robert, the Parisians could feel secure from all danger of being starved into surrender.

In spite, however, of these successes, and of the continual efforts of de Retz and Beaufort, the Parisian levies proved no match for Condé's regular troops, before whom they fled on January 23 and again on January 29. These reverses, together with the loss of Charenton on February 8, encouraged the party of moderation among the clergy and the members of the *parlement* to raise their voices in favour of peace. The people in Paris were becoming weary of the war, resented the sufferings to which they were subject, and complained of the conduct of their generals. From being a determined stand for liberties and reforms, the war was already showing signs of degenerating into a mere selfish struggle on the part of the nobles against the centralisation of the royal power, and especially against Mazarin.

In many respects the siege of 1649 foreshadowed that of 1870. There was the same levity and anarchy, the same endurance and courage. Condé and Moltke both experienced similar difficulties in their attempts to subdue the French capital. Through the influence of de Retz negotiations were entered into with Spain, and a Spanish envoy arrived in Paris. But a reaction had begun, and the moderate party in the *parlement* protested against dealings with Spain. The clergy favoured a settlement, and the news of the execution of Charles I. shocked the consciences of the more reasonable men on both sides. The loss, too, on February 25, of the town of Brie-Comte-Robert increased enormously the difficulty of securing supplies. Though de Retz remained master of the Parisian populace, and intractable, and though the nobles of the Fronde stood aloof, moderate counsels prevailed, and on February 28 the *parlement* decided to send deputies, who should treat not with Mazarin, but with the court. The interests of the royal cause demanded a settlement, even though of a temporary character. Turenne was still anxious to march to the aid of Paris, the Archduke Leopold was ready to invade France, and some of the French governors of frontier towns were intriguing with the Spaniards. Concessions were therefore 'advisable. On March 11 a compromise was patched up, known as the Treaty of Rueil. But in Paris the terms were refused. The extreme members of the *parlement* were furious when they realised that Mazarin was to remain in power, and that, till the end of 1649, the *parlement* was not to discuss political questions. It was not till April 2 that the treaty, slightly modified, was accepted, and the twelve weeks' war came to an end. The right of the *parlement* to take some part in State affairs was reluctantly allowed by Mazarin, and the treaty was registered ; the Parisian troops were then disbanded. But the main object of the Frondeurs, the expulsion of Mazarin from France, remained unfulfilled, and the people and nobles regarded the treaty with no enthusiasm   Though, however, the Parisian populace might cry "No peace ! No Mazarin !" the merchants were anxious for peace without delay, and the queen-regent realised that the restoration of the royal authority depended on the continued presence of Mazarin at the head of the government. Nevertheless the struggle was not yet over. Though Paris was illuminated, and a *Te Deum* chanted, men like de Retz and Beaufort remained hostile. The Treaty of Rueil was merely a truce.

CARDINAL MAZARIN

THE EARLY YEARS OF THE NEW FRONDE

The Treaty of Rueil neither excited enthusiasm among the French people nor did it allay the troubles in the provinces. In Provence and Normandy there had been disturbances, which in the former province continued, while in Guienne the discontent had developed into something approaching rebellion. The Duke of Epernon, the governor of that province, had, by his tyranny,

stirrecb up disorders which were with difficulty only partly suppressed. The re-establishment of the intendants was requisite for the preservation of order and good government, and Mazarin, though unable at that time to carry out this very necessary measure, hit upon the plan of sending members of the parliamentary families as commissioners into the provinces. He thus did something to remedy one of the chief blunders of the Chamber of St. Louis.

The First or Old Fronde had had disastrous results upon the provincial administration. Its effects upon the course of the war against Spain were equally detrimental. Hoping to gain advantageous terms from Mazarin owing to the troubles in Paris, the Spaniards refused to consent to the cession of Alsace, or to make peace without receiving large concessions. The French position in Italy, Catalonia, and Flanders had been indeed weakened, and the Archduke Leopold had succeeded in taking Saint Venant (April 25, 1649) and Ypres (May 10) ; but Mazarin had shown no signs of relinquishing any portion of what France had won by the Peace of Westphalia, and the event fully justified him.

For some time, however, the situation on the north-east border remained a source of serious anxiety. Condé had declined to take command of the army, and

Turenne, though outwardly reconciled to the court, remained, like his brother the Duke of Bouillon, hostile to Mazarin, and refused to undertake the siege of Cambray. The seizure of the principality of Sedan by Richelieu still rankled in the minds of Bouillon and Turenne, and Mazarin so far had been unable to satisfy their ambition and win them over to the side of the crown by offers of territory and pensions. Harcourt, the commander in Flanders, did, indeed, endeavour to second Mazarin's statesmanlike efforts to restore the French fortunes, but he failed to capture Cambray, and this reverse was a source of congratulation to the unpatriotic enemies of the court, and a fresh series of Mazarinades appeared, some of a most insulting character. Mazarin at once proceeded to Saint-Quentin to encourage Harcourt, who, early in September, took Condé, a place of considerable importance. Though later on compelled to abandon thb town, he had, at any rate, shown the Spaniards that France was still able to carry out an offensive policy on the frontier.

On August 18, 1649, the court returned to Paris. Mazarin had gained over the Duchess of Chevreuse, but had failed to conciliate de Retz or Beaufort. Nevertheless", the arrival of the king and court was the signal for great rejoicings in Paris, and to outward appearance internal peace was assured. Even Mazarin had no unfriendly reception. But already signs of the formation of a new Fronde were not wanting. The party of the *Importants,* who in 1643 had been swept away by Mazarin, were again raising their heads, and they hoped to find a leader in Condé. This new Fronde, unlike the Parliamentary Fronde, entertained no serious projects of reform. It was mainly composed of the princes and their followers, young nobles known as *petits maîtres;* it was a struggle of ambition; it was an endeavour to overthrow Mazarin. The New Frondeurs had no popular sympathies ; they felt no respect for the *parlement* of Paris. They lived in an atmosphere of intrigue ; they aimed at securing power for themselves.

Turbulent, insolent, intriguing, and unpatriotic, the New Fronde has no claim to any sympathy or respect. A remarkable feature in the New Fronde was the influence exercised by ladies. Even during the period of the Old Fronde the Duchess of Longueville and other high-born ladies had taken a leading part against the court. But the lawyers, headed by Molé, had kept some control over the movement, and had closed the war by the Peace of Rueil. During the New Fronde the *parlement* was compelled to subordinate its feebly-expressed wishes to the loud demands of the brilliant galaxy of ladies who for some three years influenced politics in a remarkable fashion. " Women," says Lavallée in his *Histoire des Français,*" played throughout this time the most splendid part, which brought out all their cleverness ; theirs was a life of adventure and romance, crowded with pleasures and perils ; they took the lead alike in love affairs or warlike expeditions, in fêtes or conspiracies. . . ." Women had frequently played a conspicuous part in French politics, but probably never had they enjoyed so much influence in the State as during the period of the New Fronde. That influence exercised by these beautiful, witty, and dissolute duchesses was generally baneful, and opposed to the true interests of France. Lavallée's judgment is not too severe. " When," he says, " they " (the ladies) "chose to play a part in politics, they brought into public affairs their sordid passions, their narrow views, their frivolous ideas, and they sacrificed to their vanity their honour, their own peace of mind, and the welfare of their houses."

Condé's own character fitted him for the post of leader. His greed for power and pelf, his arrogance, his instability and lawlessness, mark him out a man who would in his own interests endeavour to secure the supreme influence in the State even with Spanish aid. A brilliant soldier, with many of the gifts of a great general, as are evidenced by the tactics of Rocroi and Lens, Condé had no political wisdom, and his conduct from the time of the return of the court to Paris in August 1649 admits of no excuse. His unpatriotic action in allying with Spain and fighting against his own country cannot be justified on any grounds.

This was the man whose demands Mazarin in the autumn of 1649 had to satisfy. Condé had won brilliant victories for the regent ; he had, on behalf of the court, vanquished the Parliamentary Fronde. For these services he did not consider that, he had been adequately recompensed. He was, moreover, furious at Mazarin's wise refusal to hand over to Longueville Pont de l'Arche in Normandy. Jealous of the rival house of Vendôme, he opposed the marriage of Laura Mancini, one of Mazarin's nieces, to the Duke of Mercceur, son of the Duke of Vendôme. Mazarin had no doubt hoped to gain over the Duke of Beaufort through his brother Mercceur, and to oppose to the house of Condé the powerful house of Vendôme. As it was, Condé's opposition in September to the marriage brought matters to a head, and all Mazarin's enemies gathered round the prince. To avoid the immediate outbreak of hostilities, Mazarin had recourse to diplomacy. On October 2 he signed a document which seemed to hand over all authority to the prince. By this success Condé alienated the Frondeurs, who accused him of deserting their cause. The populace of Paris had not forgotten that he headed the besieging army. By seizing the supreme power he had reduced the king to a puppet, and rendered himself unendurable to the queen-regent and Mazarin. The great nobles of France were jealous of the influence and power grasped at by Condé, who had in vain supported the Duchess of Longueville's attempt to secure for two of her friends the *tabouret,* or right of being seated in the queen's presence. An uneasy period ensued in which the prince endeavoured to render his position independent of the crown, and in which his insolence and tyranny became more and more accentuated.

He had mortally offended Anne of Austria ; he had alarmed the *parlement,* which realised that it had less to fear from the court than from Condé and his following ; he was disliked by the citizens ; and, what was of immediate importance, he was not supported by de Retz.

The coadjutor, who during these times played so brilliantly the rôle of party leader, would willingly have ousted Mazarin from his position. Unable to carry out this wish, he had posed as a mighty demagogue, and was proud of his influence over the Paris mob. Fearing the tyranny of Condé, he was now prepared to unite with Mazarin in delivering the court from the new danger which threatened it. In January 1650 Mazarin determined to free himself and the court from the man who not only had extorted terms which made him virtual master of France, but who was now inciting the *parlement* of Bordeaux to rebellion, and was endeavouring to secure a hold upon Normandy. Fortunately, as we have seen, Condé, by his arrogance, had broken with de Retz, Beaufort, and generally with the Old Fronde. Mazarin, who was supported by Orleans, and who had won over Beaufort by elaborate promises, was thus able to effect a union with de Retz, to whom a cardinal's hat was promised.

A *coup d'état* was planned and carried out. On January 10, 1650, Condé, Conti, and Longueville were arrested and shut up in the chateau of Vincennes. The *parlement* made no objection, Paris remained quiet, the authority of the regent was restored. In alliance with the

Old Fronde Mazarin had temporarily checkmated the New Fronde. But the friends of the imprisoned princes at once endeavoured to raise rebellion in the provinces, and in this work the influence of women was very apparent. In fact, throughout the New or Second Fronde the influence of the great court ladies is often more effective than that of the men. The Duchesses of Longueville and of Chevreuse, Mazarin once said, could overthrow ten States. The former (Condé's sister) now endeavoured to raise Normandy ; but failing, fled to Stenay, where she met and stirred up Turenne to fresh unpatriotic acts.

Mazarin had little difficulty in establishing the royal authority in Normandy. On February 1 the court proceeded to that province. Eieppe yielded, and after some negotiations the Duke of Richelieu gave up Havre. That worthy was the grand-nephew of the great cardinal, and his wife, Anne Poussart du Vigean, was entirely in the hands of Condé and the Duchess of Longueville. By his marriage Richelieu had fallen under Condé's influence, and it had been feared that he would refuse to yield Havre. The grant of the *tabouret* to his wife, however, removed all difficulties, and a heavy bribe led to the submission of the château of Caen by its commander, who held it in the name of the Duke of

Longueville. Saint-Lô, Cherbourg, and Granville were without any resistance placed by Francis de Matignon in the hands of the cardinal, who showed great skill in the adoption of measures to ensure the tranquillity and prosperity of Normandy. On February 20, bringing in its train the Duke and Duchess of Richelieu and other hostages, the court left Normandy, and on the following day arrived in Paris. Early in March the same process was repeated in Burgundy where Condé was governor. Before starting on his journey Mazarin had realised the existence of a perfect network of intrigues in Paris, of which Orleans was the nominal centre. The members of the Old Fronde, with which Mazarin was still in alliance, were as grasping as ever, and the Duchess of Chevreuse distinguished herself by the number and extent of her demands. It was with considerable misgiving that Mazarin again began the work of pacification. From March 5 to March 16, when the court arrived at Dijon, Mazarin was to a great extent occupied in correspondence with le Tellier, his trusted agent in Paris, with reference to the constant intrigues which the weakness of Orleans encouraged. De Retz refused to be satisfied with an abbey, but for a time the house of Vendôme ceased its active opposition.

In Burgundy the centre of resistance was Bellegarde, where were concentrated many of Condé's partisans. The presence of the young king on the lines was hailed by the garrison with cries of "Vive le Roi." Mazarin's estimate of the depth of French loyalty was correct, and the moderation of his terms statesmanlike.

On April 11, Bellegarde yielded, and Mazarin's hands were free to deal with the intrigue in the capital and the revolt in Guienne. Both in Paris and in Guienne a sudden and unfavourable turn in events, "fraught with important results to Condé and France," had taken place, due to the influence of Claire-Clemence de Maillé, the hitherto despised wife of the imprisoned prince. The dowager Princess of Condé had perpetual and close relations with her son's partisans in Paris and the provinces; while her daughter-in-law, with her son Enghien, now showed unexpected energy, escaped from Chantilly, and after a short stay at Montrond, made their way to the south. There, owing to Épernon's unpopularity, to the intrigues of the dowager Princess of Condé, and the hope of Spanish assistance, rebellion had broken out, and Bordeaux became again the centre of disloyalty. Turenne, still under the influence of the Duchess of Longueville, held Stenay against the French, though the *parlement* of Paris had, on May 16, declared him, the duchess, and Rochefoucauld guilty of high treason. No immediate harm came from the Spanish alliance, as, though the Spaniards captured Le Catelet on June 15, they failed to take the citadel of Guise, and on July 1 retired from the town. Mazarin himself had no fear of a march of the Spanish forces upon Paris. He was convinced that Turenne's alliance with Spain was half-hearted, and that the Spaniards, as soon as the south of France was pacified, would content themselves with attacking towns on the north-east frontier. He therefore decided to proceed with the court to Guienne.

Mazarin's decision was rendered necessary by the certainty that the *parlements* of Toulouse and Aix were prepared to imitate the rebellious example of that of Bordeaux. He feared too that the existence of intrigues of Bordeaux with Spain and England might have serious results. On July 4 the court left Paris, and early in August a deputation from the *parlement* of Bordeaux was received. The execution of the governor of the château of Vayres led to the breaking off of negotiations, and to reprisals on the part of the Bordelais. The war therefore took a vindictive and sanguinary character. The city was full of Condé's partisans, it was the centre of a district always celebrated for its independent character, it was known later as the headquarters of the Girondist movement. The populace in the autumn of 1650 soon became supreme and declared "for the cause of the princes." It was of the utmost importance to Mazarin that the rising should be suppressed as quickly as possible. In Italy matters were going badly for the French. Porto Longone and Piombino had fallen, and the Spanish fleet, now supreme in the Mediterranean, could sail to the help of Bordeaux. Conspiracies had been discovered in Normandy, while on the north-east frontier the Spaniards had taken La Capelle, Vervins, and Marie, and Turenne had seized Bethel and Château-Porcien. Paris itself was in danger, and measures of defence were taken. It was decided to remove the princes to some more distant prison. On August 29 they were taken to Marcoussis, and thus Turenne was deprived of his principal motive for marching on the capital. The effects, however, of the disasters to the French arms were serious, and the enemies of Mazarin in Paris charged the cardinal with all the responsibility of the defeats on the frontier.

During the absence of the court in the south of France, the government in Paris had been carried on by a council which included Châteauneuf, the keeper of the seals, le Tellier, Servien, the Count of Avaux, and had for its president Orleans. The *parlement* had at once begun to discuss the complaints of the inhabitants of Bordeaux and the imprisonment of the princes, and Orleans showed no capacity for ruling. He fell under the influence of the Duchess of Chevreuse, of his wife, and of Madlle. de Saugeon. The Spaniards opened negotiations withvhim, and de Retz urged him to seize the government and direct the affairs of the country. While Orleans was falling under these pernicious influences, Châteauneuf was busy scheming to supplant Mazarin—whom he openly denounced—in his position as First Minister. The policy of trusting Orleans had succeeded no better than that of balancing the two houses of Orleans and Condé against each other. It was necessary to take steps to defeat the machinations of the Frondeurs in Paris, and Mazarin therefore had every reason to act energetically at Bordeaux, in order to be free to return to Paris. La Meilleraye, who commanded the royal forces, met with a fierce resistance, and in order to get his hands free Mazarin offered the Bordelais excellent terms. These were accepted on September 29, and the king and court entered Bordeaux on October 5.

Before returning to Paris, Mazarin made efforts to secure the allegiance of the Count of Alais, governor of Provence. The count was a zealous supporter of Condé, and the chances of the outbreak of a civil war in Provence were considerable. No rebellion, however, broke out, and having captured

Montrond, the king and court arrived at Fontainebleau on November 8.

Mazarin had now become weary of the incessant intrigues in Paris. Successful against the parties of the princes, he proposed to inflict a decisive defeat upon the Spaniards, and then to deal with his enemies in Paris. He was resolved to resist the demands of the Duchess of Chevreuse for money and places, and that of de Retz for a cardinal's hat. The Spaniards were already masters of part of Champagne, and it was absolutely necessary to drive them from Rethel—a strategic point of much importance, closing as it did the valley of the Upper Aisne. It could be easily provisioned, and a Spanish army in possession of it would be a perpetual menace to Paris. Before starting on the campaign, which it was hoped would be crowned with success, Mazarin secured the assent of Orleans to the removal of the princes to

Havre. This effected, he joined the army on the frontier in December. Rethel was taken on the 13th, and on the 15th Turenne was defeated in a pitched battle near the town. Champagne was cleared of the Spaniards, and the value of the royal troops had been proved. Mazarin never showed his wisdom more clearly than in his efforts to provide for the army and keep it loyal. On the day of the battle of Rethel he sent provisions, wine, and medical necessaries for the wounded. In the future the king could always count upon his army. Mazarin could with some justice look back upon the events of 1650. "It began," he wrote to one of his correspondents, "with the imprisonment of the princes; then took place the journeys to Normandy, Burgundy, and

Guienne ; and finally there were the events in Champagne, whence I have driven the enemy in the middle of winter, after having recovered Rethel and many other important places. Lastly, there is the battle which resulted in the loss of the enemy's army." To all appearance Mazarin had cause for his satisfaction. The party of the princes had lost control of Normandy, Burgundy, Saumur, Guienne, and Montrond. Turenne had been defeated and the power of the crown fully vindicated. Mazarin, who had in November appointed

Nicholas Fouquet, one of his most trusted agents, *procureur-général,* returned to Paris on December 31, 1650. From that time he gradually carried out a project the wisdom of which circumstances had made evident to him. That project implied the formation of a monarchical and national party which should stand above faction. The basis of such a party would be the *bourgeoisie,* which was already wearied of the struggles of the Frondes. But this plan, though excellent, was premature, and years had to elapse before it could be carried out.

Paris was seething with intrigue, Mazarin was hated by all parties, the *parlement* had discovered that the arrest of Condé was contrary to law, and de Retz, furious at not obtaining a cardinal's hat, had no difficulty in stirring up the capital.

During the First Fronde Mazarin and the queen had been supported by Condé, and, since the imprisonment of the latter, by Orleans. De Retz had now secured the alliance of Orleans, and the union of the two Frondes against Mazarin left the court practically defenceless. The question naturally arises, Could not Mazarin have taken severe measures and suppressed by force of arms the factions in Paris? That was the view of Lionne, afterwards celebrated as a diplomatist, and now one of Mazarin's supporters. At the beginning of 1651 Mazarin could adopt one of two courses—either reconciliation with one of the two factions opposed to him, and with its aid to overthrow the other ; or the declaration of war upon both. There are indications that Mazarin strongly inclined to the latter course—that he relied on the army to suppress the factions which troubled France. Before, however, declaring war upon de Retz and his followers, it would be necessary for the queen to leave Paris. Unfortunately, Anne of Austria was laid up with an illness which had attacked her at Poitiers and again at Amboise. Mazarin himself wrote to Servien that he was prevented from carrying out the second alternative, which was the best, " par une fatalité qui a rendu la reine malade dans cette conjoncture, et hors d'état de pouvoir peut-être de plus d'un mois tenter ce coup." His enforced hesitation at this crisis had disastrous results. Before he could build up a national party and suppress the factions by force of arms, Paris and Bordeaux experienced revolution and a period of civil war.

During January 1651, while Mazarin hesitated, his enemies, headed by de Retz, acted with decision. The *parlement* declared itself openly and strongly in favour of the princes, and the two Frondes united. Mazarin, who had thought himself, after Rethel, able to vanquish the two Frondes, had miscalculated his strength. He now appears to have been somewhat taken by surprise, and adopted no decisive measures. The link which bound him to Orleans was finally broken on February 1, 1651, when the duke, who had joined de Retz and Beaufort in declaring that the liberty of the princes was necessary for the welfare of the State, stated to Anne of Austria that the Frondeurs were simply attacking the deplorable policy of Mazarin. The cardinal, on the other hand, said that the Frondeurs, like Fairfax and Cromwell, wished, while attacking the minister, to destroy the royal power. Recognising, however, that hostility to himself was the bond of union between the two factions, Mazarin decided to withdraw. On February 6, 1651, he left Paris. The queen having been prevented on February 9 from following his example (her attempt somewhat resembling that of Louis XVI. in 1791 to go to Saint-Cloud), she was compelled to give orders for the release of the princes. On hearing this news, Mazarin at once proceeded to Havre, and on February 13 set the princes at liberty. He apparently hoped, though in vain, to gain their gratitude. In March he left France, and from April

11 to the end of October he lived at Brühl. During this period he was in constant communication with the— queen, le Tellier, Lionne, Servien, who were, with Nicholas Fouquet, his most trusted supporters. Under his direction Anne of Austria carried on a ceaseless war with her enemies, and by following his advice was able to triumph eventually over her foes.

" The return of the princes to Paris was a veritable triumph," and was followed by measures for perpetuating the victory of the aristocracy over the monarchy. The *parlement* at once annulled all declarations directed against any of Condé's supporters, and a small committee, consisting of Orleans, Condé, de Retz, and Beaufort, met to direct affairs. For a time matters looked black for the cause of royalty in France. Both Frondes were united, the *parlement* and the nobles were in full accord, the assembly of the clergy declared itself for liberty and Condé. To preserve the union between the parties of Orleans and Condé a double marriage was arranged. Enghien, Condé's son, was to marry a daughter of Orleans, and Conti was to marry the daughter of the Duchess of Chevreuse. The united houses of Orleans and Condé, with their powerful sup-porters, and aided by the connections and friends of the Duchess of Chevreuse, would, it was confidently believed, be too powerful for any combination which Anne of Austria could bring against it. The hopes of the triumphant princes were high, and drastic changes in the government of France were contemplated. The nobles and clergy were disposed to summon the States-General, and by its means to make serious modifications in the constitution. The regency was to be taken from Anne of Austria, and a council of eighteen, chosen from the Three Estates, was to be formed for the government of the country.

Such was the situation which Anne of Austria, who was practically a prisoner in the Palais-Royal, had to face in the early months of the year 1651. When roused she could act with determination, and Anne was as firmly resolved as ever to defend the rights of the yoking king. Ready and anxious to combat the proposed revolution, she was encouraged in her resistance by the constant advice of Mazarin, and by the devotion of his agents, Servien and Lionne, who remained in Paris, and with whom Mazarin regularly corresponded. The cardinal was much disturbed on hearing of the union of the princes with the Old Fronde. He showed, however, no sign of despair, but advised the queen-mother to take all precautions to prevent the abduction of the king, and to seize every opportunity of sowing discord among the princes. He was confident that the coalition would before long break up into its original elements. Aware that the *parlement* would view with horror the proposal to summon the States-General, he advised Anne not to reject the proposition of the nobles and clergy, but to defer the meeting of the Three Estates till after the king had attained his majority.

Events turned out as Mazarin anticipated. A violent quarrel ensued between the magistrates and the nobles, while the clergy resented the proposal of the *parlement* to exclude all cardinals from the royal council. The exile of Mazarin had by no means produced peace among all classes. Dissensions prevailed among the Frondeurs, and the queen felt strong enough to refuse, at the request of Orleans, to dismiss le Tellier, Servien, and Lionne. She also entered into secret negotiations with Condé, in accordance with Mazarin's advice to sow discord between Orleans and Condé. In this she was aided by the return of the Duchess of Longueville to Paris. This lady had for years hated the Duchesses of Chevreuse and Montbazon, and her rage was great on discovering that it had been arranged that the daughter of the former should marry her brother Conti. By her efforts the proposed marriage never took place, and the rupture of the engagement distinctly weakened the bonds between Condé and the party of Orleans. Condé was, however, for the moment all-powerful.

To dissolve the union of the parties of Condé and Orleans, Anne, by the advice of Mazarin, had entered into an intrigue with Condé against Châteauneuf, *le garde des sceaux,* who was one of Orleans' supporters. Condé, who was promised Guienne instead of Burgundy, agreed to the exclusion of Châteauneuf from the Council, and to the admission of Chavigny and Molé, who had been suggested by Mazarin. On April 3, 1651, Anne carried out a veritable *coup d'état.* A ministerial revolution was effected, and Châteauneuf was disgraced. Though civil war, owing to the rage of the Orleans faction, almost broke out, peace was maintained, and Condé's influence in the Council was assured. The rupture of the Chevreuse marriage scheme was an accomplished fact before the end of April, and the two factions had become irreconcilable. Condé, however, soon ruined his cause by his extravagant actions and arrogant conduct. He was resolved to remain supreme, and to secure the preponderance in the State of his own family and friends.

One of the principal results of the rupture of the f union between the two Frondes was the improved position of Anne of Austria and of Louis XIV. They were no longer prisoners in the Palais-Royal, and even appeared publicly in Notre Dame. This change in the situation was largely due to Mazarin's counsels, which Anne of Austria had followed with precision ; and she had also secured valuable support from Anne of Gonzagua, the Princess Palatine. This remarkable woman was one of the heroines of the New Fronde, and like the Duchesses of Longueville and Chevreuse was rapacious and ambitious. Nevertheless she proved a useful ally, and by her efforts contributed in great measure to detach Condé from the Old Fronde and from the influence of the Duchess of Chevreuse. In her negotiations with Condé she had been ably seconded by Servien and Lionne, who, according to'Mazarin, went beyond his instructions in their offers to Condé. Had the latter's ambitious hopes been satisfied, he would have controlled the south-west of France, and by his enormous influence would have seriously curtailed the power of Louis XIV. Successful in breaking up the alliance between the parties of Condé and of Orleans, Anne of Austria's next step was to defeat the schemes of Condé.

Both Mazarin and the queen were determined to resist the exorbitant pretensions of this overgrown subject, who seemed for a time to be master of events.

Holding Guienne, Condé would be a real menace and danger to the State. As soon as Mazarin was convinced that Condé's triumph meant the annihilation of the royal power, he advised the queen to continue her efforts to sow dissension between the prince and his allies. The *parlement* was alienated by Condé's arrogance, his manner in the Council was insulting, even his own relations were weary of his haughtiness. His brother-in-law, the Duke of Longueville, had no wish to be involved in any more plots, and was on bad terms with his wife, Condé's sister. Turenne, too, and his brother, the Duke of Bouillon, were irritated with him, as they had not received the principality of Sedan, the object of their wishes for many years, and were prepared to listen to the overtures of Mazarin.

Molé, one of the most faithful of the prince's partisans, had now detached himself from him, and the

Dukes of Nemours and of Joyeuse, together with the Marshals la Mothe and la Meilleraye, were discontented. The Duchess of Chevreuse, with the Marquis of Châteauneuf, was again ready to treat with Mazarin, and even de Retz was willing to come to terms. The rumour of the return of Mazarin, however, was sufficient to throw the *parlement* into a panic. It was necessary to move cautiously. At the end of June 1651 Louis of Vendôme, Duke of Mercceur, married Laura Mancini, one of Mazarin's nieces ; but the event, beyond irritating Beaufort, was of small importance. The opposition of so many influential Frondeurs was, however, a serious matter for Condé ; and Madame de Motteville testifies to his fear of being arrested by some of his former allies. On July 6 Condé fled to the château of Saint-Maur.

Surrounded by his friends, the question of embarking at once upon civil war was discussed, though both Bouillon and Turenne urged moderation and reconciliation with Mazarin. Negotiations were opened with Orleans, and Condé consented to return to Paris if le Tellier, Servien, and Lionne, who were rightly regarded as being devoted to Mazarin, were dismissed. On July 19 the queen yielded, and Nicholas Fouquet remained the sole faithful correspondent of Mazarin in

Paris. On July 23 Condé returned to the capital. A slight to the young king roused the monarchical sentiment among the Parisians and a feeling of indignation against Condé. By Mazarin's advice the queen allied with de Retz and his faction, the price of the alliance being a promise of a cardinal's hat to de Retz, of the post of First Minister to Châteauneuf, and of the seals to Mole. Mazarin's nephew, a Mancini, was to marry Madlle. de Chevreuse; and the Duchess of Chevreuse, Châteauneuf, and de Retz were to do all in their power to detach Orleans from Condé. Secure of the support of de Eetz and the members of the Old Fronde, the queen, on August 17, accused Condé publicly of disloyalty and of treasonable intercourse with Spain. Civil war almost ensued between the two Frondes, and was only averted owing to the approaching celebration of the king's majority. To preserve peace Anne agreed to postpone the settlement of all questions at issue till after that event; and, in order to conciliate the *parlement* and the people, did not even oppose the issue of a fierce declaration against Mazarin. The cardinal himself was appalled by the violence of the language used. But Anne of Austria had only agreed to the declaration from motives of policy. On September 7, 1651, the majority of Louis

XIY. was celebrated, and a new situation was created. Mazarin's plan for uniting all loyal *S* men in support of the king had now good chance of success. Such a scheme could alone vanquish the Frondeurs and restore peace to France. The principal obstacle to the realisation of this scheme was Condé. Rebellion or submission were now the only alternatives open to him. In an evil moment for his fame and for the welfare of his country he decided, with the full concurrence of his sister, the notorious Duchess of Longue-ville, to ally with Spain, and to involve France in civil war. Till 1653 Mazarin had to deal with an armed rebellion.

THE CLOSE OF THE FRONDE

At the time of the celebration of Louis XIV.'s majority (September 7, 1651) the king's Council included Orleans, the Marquis of Châteauneuf, who always hoped to be Mazarin's successor, Molé, and la Vieuville, superintendent of the finances. While Mazarin remained at Brühl, Condé, with his brother Conti, Nemours, Rochefoucauld, and Viole, was at Chajitilly. Already, influenced by the Duchess of Longueville, he had decided on rebellion, and the political situation of France seemed to favour his plans. Oliver Cromwell, successful in England, was disposed to foment troubles in France, if not actually to seize some of her northern ports.   Spain was bidding for an English alliance.

In the south Condé was received with enthusiasm, and the families of la Force, la Rochefoucauld, la Trémoille, and Rohan embraced his cause. Daugnon, who held the fortress of Brouage, and was governor of La Rochelle, and who hoped to form La Rochelle, with Ré and Oléron, into an independent principality, supported him. Condé's schemes were extensive. He proposed to carry the war to the Loire, to effect a junction with the Duke of Nemours, who commanded troops in the north of France, while Turenne, supreme at Stejiay, would march through Champagne and perhaps occupy Paris. The crisis was serious, for France was still split into a number of selfish, unpatriotic factions, while the almost universal hatred of Mazarin was a serious obstacle to the development of the tendency towards the triumph of the monarchy. At first the Council showed unexpected vigour. On September 26, 1651, Louis XIV. and the court left Paris for Fontainebleau, and in October proceeded with a small army into the province of Berri. Success attended the efforts of the king's party. In Saintonge, where Harcourt commanded, Cognac was relieved (November) and La Rochelle was seized, while in Berri the king occupied Bourges and established the royal authority. The court then proceeded to Poitiers. By the end of the year a considerable step had been taken towards the suppression of the rebellion. All danger from Lower Poitou had disappeared, and Daugnon had made terms with the court. Condé's hopes of seizing La Rochelle and Sajntonge were defeated, and some of his supporters urged him to make peace. Condé, however, was more obstinate than ever in his determination to secure his own supremacy. He handed over Bourg, a town in Guienne, to Spain, and the king at once sent to Paris a declaration depriving Condé of his governments and honours. He endeavoured to strengthen his position by means of new allies, and made advances to Charles IV., Duke of Lorraine. For eighteen years a duke without a duchy, this adventurer was always ready to enter into projects of any kind. All danger from the union of Lorraine with Condé was, however, removed by the intervention of Mazarin, who dangled before the duke the hope of the restitution of his duchy as a reward for his loyalty to Louis XIV. Foiled by Mazarin in his designs upon the Duke of Lorraine, Condé had also hoped to secure assistance from Oliver Cromwell. Agents from the prince proceeded to England, and it is said that Englishmen were busy trying to persuade

Bordeaux to form a republic. Condé's envoys to Cromwell were carefully watched by Mazarin's spies, and there is no doubt that Mazarin succeeded in inducing Cromwell not to support Condé. At the end of 1651 that prince could rely upon Spain alone for help in his rebellion against the French monarchy.

On January 29, 1652, Mazarin at the head of an army joined the court at Poitiers. The news of his return had caused great excitement in Paris, where the *parlement,* on December 29, a price on his head, and decreed the sale of his invaluable library. Two days after his arrival at Poitiers, Turenne and Bouillon also came to give their services to the royal cause. In place of the principality of Sedan, which Eichelieu had taken from their family, Mazarin had given them the duchies of Château-Thierry and Albret, with the counties of Evreux and Auvergne, and other domains. The value of Turenne to the king's cause was at that time immense. Troops were required for the defence of Catalonia, which had been abandoned by Marsin, one of Condé's adherents. A fleet had to be sent to Barcelona, but, above all, the revolt in Anjou required immediate suppression. De Retz received his cardinal's hat. The Council was rapidly reorganised, Châteauneuf, Mazarin's rival, retired, and an advance was then made into Anjou.

On the Loire the Frondeurs had two armies—one under Beaufort, the other under Nemours. At Jargeau, on March 29, 1652, they were defeated by Turenne. The news of the defeat of his forces brought Condé from Bordeaux to the Loire, and on April 1, at Bléneau, he defeated the royal troops. The arrival of Turenne saved the royal army from a complete disaster. " Condé," writes the Due d'Aumale, " had reached his mark, and had annihilated one of the royal armies, when the fortunate intervention of Turenne and his cool boldness and tactical skill changed the result of the day. . . . But if Condé had taken the offensive in his wonted fashion, he might perhaps have overwhelmed Turenne and found Louis XIV. on his hands." Instead of continuing the operations on the Loire, Condé hurried off to Paris to win over the Duke of Orleans and the *parlement.*

The capital was indeed incensed against Mazarin, but the *parlement* was not prepared to oppose the king, the declaration of whose majority had taken all power out of the hands of the Duke of Orleans. As Mazarin had hoped, a national party was slowly being formed among the *bourgeoisie,* who longed for peace and the establishment of order. Unable to secure support from the well-to-do classes, Condé turned to the mob and determined to stir up popular passions. This was all the easier as Turenne was close at hand with the king and Mazarin. Had Mazarin adopted Turenne's advice and boldly entered the capital and proclaimed the king, the war would probably have been ended. But Mazarin, knowing how hated he was, decided to carry on negotiations, and was supported in his decision by the queen-mother.

Meanwhile Turenne, on May 4, overthrew Condé's Spanish force at Étampes, and the effect in Paris of the news of this defeat was considerable. Anarchy increased and all government disappeared. The sudden arrival of the Duke of Lorraine with 10,000 mercenaries to relieve the town of Étampes, then besieged by Turenne, was a serious danger to the royal army. Turenne, however, by his skill averted the danger, and the duke retired to the frontier. Turenne then advanced on Paris, which during the next few months was the scene of disorder. Condé was encamped at Saint-Cloud, and on July 2, 1652, the battle of Saint-Antoine was fought. Persuaded by Mazarin and the young king to attack before his preparations were complete, Turenne was at first checked by his brilliant antagonist. When his guns had come up, the final arrangements were being made for a decisive effort. But Madlle. de Montpensier ("Mademoiselle"), the famous daughter of the Duke of Orleans, turned the guns of the Bastille upon the royal army, while Condé's force was admitted into Paris.

Scenes of violence at once took place, and on July 4 the mob, encouraged by Condé and his soldiers, set fire to the Hôtel de Ville, where the General Assembly of the city was sitting, and murdered several of the councillors. This massacre of the Hôtel de Ville, though immediately followed by the establishment of Condé's rule in Paris, was the deathblow to the party of the princes. But for a time Paris was forced to submit to a government which included Orleans as lieutenant-general of France, Condé as compander-in-chief, Beaufort governor of Paris, and Broussel provost; the monarchical party, however, daily gained strength.

In Paris the reaction steadily went on, and in August the *parlement* was ordered by the king to proceed to Pontoise. In order to remove all cause of irritation and to propitiate Paris, Mazarin, on August 19, voluntarily left the kingdom a second time. Condé's last excuse for rebellion was gone. The departure of Mazarin placed the princes in a difficult position. On August 22 they declared to the *parlement* that they were ready to lay down their arms on certain conditions. They were to be confirmed in their honours, dignities, and governments, and to be allowed to keep in their employ the troops which they had raised. At the same time they prepared to continue the civil war, and sent a pressing appeal to the Spaniards and to the Duke of Lorraine for assistance. Mazarin, who accused the Duke of Lorraine of having broken his engagements with him, at once advised an energetic opposition on the part of the royal troops to the Lorrainers.

For a time, however, it seemed that the royal cause was threatened with very real danger from its foreign enemies. Considering that the cause of Condé was not hopeless, the Archduke Leopold, governor of the Spanish Netherlands, ordered Fuensaldaña to lead a Spanish force into France, to effect a junction with the Duke of Lorraine, who was simultaneously advancing, and to march on Paris. But the Spaniards were only half-hearted, and were content to leave the parties in France to continue their intestine struggles. On Turenne's approach Fuensaldaña fell back to the frontier and besieged Dunkirk. Meanwhile the Duke of Lorraine, with from 9000 to 10,000 men, was marching on Paris. His plan was to occupy the heights of Villeneuve St. George, unite with Condé, and overwhelm Turenne's small army. Turenne, however, anticipated the duke, and during the month of September, in command of Villeneuve St. George, held in check the Lorrainers as well as Condé's forces. Had Turenne been boldly attacked he would, in all probability, have been defeated by his more powerful enemies. But Condé, perhaps through illness, showed no decision, and Lorraine, a (mere adventurer) had no liking for a pitched battle. The Bourbon monarchy was once more saved from imminent danger. Early in October Lorraine's army disappeared, and that of Condé did nothing. But the results of the unpatriotic conduct of the princes were far-reaching. The country round Paris had been devastated, and the devotion of a portion of the *bourgeoisie* and peasants for their allies gave way to a desire for a settled government and protection from devastation and disorder. In fact, the hatred felt for the Lorrainers was such that the duke could only at great risk visit Paris.   On October 12 he narrowly escaped being

murdered by the mob. A more serious result of the

continuance of the civil strife was the loss of Dunkirk. The Spaniards had wisely pushed on their operations against the town with vigour, and in August had increased the number of their troops. The French fleet had been scattered by Blake, the English admiral, and Dunkirk capitulated on September 16. Having already retaken Gravelines and Mardyke, the Spaniards had every hope of continuing their successes. "It is impossible," , wrote Mazarin, " to prevent these misfortunes if the French continue to act against France."

The cause of the princes was, however, rapidly declining. Montrond, their principal fortress in the centre of France, was lost to them early in September. During that month, between the rival forces of Turenne and Lorraine, negotiations were proceeding, all of which lay in the direction of the triumph of the monarchy. There was no reason for prolonging the period of unrest, and all classes in Paris agreed to urge the king to return. The *parlement,* the merchants, the artisans were united on this point, and the Cardinal de Retz was found among a deputation to Saint-Germain to beg Louis to enter his capital. On October 13 the Duke of Lorraine led his forces away, and Condé shortly afterwards retired with a small force to join the Spaniards. On October 14 Beaufort was removed from his post of governor of Paris. The way was now prepared for the return of the court, and on October 21, 1652, Louis entered Paris amid a scene of wild enthusiasm. An amnesty was at once passed for all the events which had occurred since February 1651, and all decrees during that period, including those attacking Mazarin, were annulled.

Orleans retired to Blois and ceased to be of any political importance, and his daughter " Mademoiselle " was exiled to Saint-Fargeau. The Duchesses of Montbazon and Châtillon were also compelled to leave Paris, and Châteauneuf was ordered to retire to Berri. On October 22, the day after the return of the court, Louis held a *lit de justice,* and forbade the *parlement* of Paris to take any part in affairs of State. Beaufort, Broussel, and nine other prominent members of the *parlement* were banished, and it was seen that no effective resistance was possible. The Bastille was next secured, and on December 19 de Retz was arrested and imprisoned in Vincennes. As far as Paris was concerned the Fronde movement was over.

The return of Mazarin was, however, absolutely

necessary. The foreign policy of France demanded his presence. The relations of the government of Louis XIV. with England, Germany, and Italy required careful handling, and French interests abroad were suffering through the absence of the cardinal. The Spaniards had in October regained Barcelona and Cásale, and had secured the alliance of the Duke of Mantua. Oliver Cromwell's attitude had become so threatening that Mazarin had persuaded Anne of Austria, in spite of the opposition of Henrietta Maria, to recognise in December the English Commonwealth, and to send Bordeaux as ambassador to London. France was also in continual danger from invasion on her eastern border, where Condé had in November seized Château-Porcien, Rethel, Sainte-Ménehould, Bar-le-Duc, Ligny, and the town of Commercy. In December, however, Mazarin succeeded in bringing reinforcements to Turenne, and Bar-le-Duc, Ligny, and Commercy were easily regained by the French. Mazarin was now ready to accede to the wishes of the queen-mother, the king, and Servien, and to return. On January 12, 1653, Château-Porcien was retaken by the French, and at the end of the month Mazarin left the army and proceeded to Soissons. On February 3, 1653, in company with the king, who had met him some miles outside the city, Mazarin entered Paris.

The state of the finances required Mazarin's immediate attention. On January 2, 1653, la Vieuville, the superintendent of finance, had died, and Nicholas Fouquet immediately applied for the pQst. Other applicants appeared—Servien, Molé, and le Tellier. Mazarin came to a characteristic decision. Richelieu had laid it down that it was impossible for two men mutually jealous to appropriate State funds. Mazarin resolved to put into force this opinion. On February 7, 1653, Servien and Fouquet were nominated jointly to the post. Till Servien's death in 1659 there were thus two superintendents of finance. In undertaking, in addition to his duties as *procureur-général,* the responsibilities of this new office, Fouquet was embarking upon a dangerous if lucrative course. The finances were in a hopeless condition. The social and political upheaval caused by the Fronde had not yet subsided ; the struggle with Spain still continued. All the avenues to new loans were closed. The practical bankruptcy of the government in 1648 had destroyed its credit, and no one could be found willing to lend money. Only through the personal credit of Mazarin or of Fouquet could the State induce men to lend money. Such a method of raising loans had obvious disadvantages. Public and private money became involved in extraordinary confusion, and many loopholes for adverse criticism soon appeared. Colbert, who had the management of Mazarin's private estate, and who aspired to a high position in the State, had already quarrelled with Fouquet and was his declared enemy. Though he continued to warn Mazarin, the minister found that Fouquet's ability to raise money from rich capitalists was invaluable. At first, however, the system of having two superintendents did not work well, and it was not till after a change had been made at the end of 1654 that men lent willingly.

Mazarin's success had been largely due to the military qualities of Turenne, to the support of his subordinates, to the loyal aspirations of the *bourgeoisie,* and to the divisions among the nobles. It was important to unite all parties round the throne and to end the war. Turenne was deservedly covered with honours, and to the house of Bouillon were given the duchies of Albret and Château-Thierry, and the counties of Auvergne, Evreux, and Gisors. In 1660 the marshal was given the title of grand-captain to distinguish him from the other generals. Mazarin, like Richelieu, preferred to employ men of the middle class ; and though he recognised the value of such men as Nicholas and Basil Fouquet, who were respectively superintendent of the finance and head of the police, he had more confidence in the honesty of le Tellier, Abel Servien, Hugh Lionne, and Jean-Baptiste Colbert. To these men Mazarin gave honours and titles freely, and not infrequently valuable emoluments. He was wise in doing so. It was by the aid of this devoted band of counsellors that he was able

to establish his power, win over the nobles, keep the *parlement* and clergy in order and conciliate the *bourgeoisie.*

With the *bourgeoisie* of Paris Mazarin soon cultivated excellent relations. The obligations of the government were recognised, order was as far as possible preserved in the streets, and literary men were paid to praise both king and minister. Mazarin was fully cognisant of the power of the press, and till his death numerous writers received pecuniary assistance from him. Being till 1659 involved in a war with Spain, Mazarin was unable, in accordance with Colbert's wish, to found trading companies, and generally to encourage the growth of a merchant marine. With the *parlement*

Mazarin's relations were on a more delicate footing, and it was more difficult to conciliate the lawyers than to win over the citizens. For many years the *parlement* had been the sworn foe of the cardinal, who had done his best to curtail its exaggerated claims and absurd pretensions. By the lavish use of bribery, however, Mazarin won over to the royal side many of the members of the *parlement,* and he procured the nomination of Pomponne de Belliévre as president in succession to Molé, who retired in March 1653. The efforts of Belliévre, who was supported by Nicholas Fouquet, the *procureur-général,* had beneficial effects, and the latent opposition of the *parlement* to the government did not cause Mazarin much anxiety.

With the clergy and religious orders the cardinal had little difficulty. The supporters of the government were liberally rewarded ; the Cardinal Antonio Barberini becoming Bishop of Poitiers, and in 1657 Archbishop of Rheims. The religious orders, such as the Franciscans and the Jesuits, were for the most part devoted to the royal cause, and Mazarin found their support useful during his contests with his old enemy Innocent X.

The nobles after 1652 gave Mazarin little trouble.

Vanquished and guilty of treason, they hastened to make abject submission to the government. La Porte gives several amusing instances to illustrate the rapidity of the conversion of the upper orders. " Tout le monde," he says, " disait tout haut à la reine que toute la France était Mazarine." And in describing the manner in which the crowd did reverence to the cardinal, he says, "J'y vis un religieux qui se prosterna devant lui avec tant d'humilité, que je crus qu'il ne s'en relèverait point."

Mazarin had experienced the value of the support of the fickle *noblesse,* and he had for a long time past determined to consolidate his power and firmly to establish his influence by bringing about marriages between his nieces and members of the principal families in France. His policy was in a way somewhat similar to the family settlement policy of some of the Plantagenets. In 1651 the Duke of Mercœur, the eldest son of the Duke of Vendôme, and one of the leading nobles in France, had married Laura Mancini. From the year 1650 Mazarin had wished to marry another niece to the eldest son of the Duke of Bouillon, so as to remove the irritation of the duke and his brother, Marshal Turenne, owing to the loss of Sedan by their family. On August 9, 1652, the Duke of Bouillon died, and later his son, the young Duke Godefroi-Maurice de la Tour, married Maria-Anna Mancini, the youngest of Mazarin's nieces. Anna-Maria Martinozzi had a varied career. Mazarin had intended that she should marry the Duke of

Cándale, the son of the Duke of Épernon. But the duke was unwilling to make what he regarded as a mesalliance, and Anna-Maria Martinozzi in February 1G54 married the Prince of Conti. In May 1653 there arrived from Rome, in company with Mazarin's two sisters, Mesdames Mancini and Martinozzi, three more nieces, Maria, Hortensia, and Maria-Anna, together with their brother, Philip Mancini. For these suitable marriages were arranged. Hortensia in 1661 married the Duke of Meilleraye, the nephew of Richelieu, who became the Duke of Mazarin and one of the heirs of the cardinal. In 1657 Olympia Mancini married Eugene of Savoy, Count of Soissons, and became the mother of Prince Eugene, so famous in the Spanish Succession War. By these marriages Mazarin secured a hold on several of the noble families in France. At the beginning of 1653 the only great houses which were openly hostile to him were those of Orleans, Condé, la Trémoille, and Harcourt. The Count of Harcourt, the head of the fourth branch of the house of Lorraine, had entered into treasonable relations with the Emperor, and had threatened to hand over to him the important town of Breisach.

But Mazarin's diplomacy came to his aid, and Harcourt was induced to submit. Orleans and his daughter were now powerless, the influence of Condé was destroyed, and la Trémoille, who was governor of Charleville, was won over by means of the Duchess of Chevreuse. The governors of strong places in the north of France had already proved their fidelity, and the governors of the principal provinces, such as Longueville in Normandy, la Meilleraye in Brittany, Mercceur in Provence, Épernon

in Burgundy, l'Hôpital in Champagne, and Lesdiguières in Dauphiné, were loud in protesting their loyalty. By his skill and moderation Mazarin had thus conciliated the *bourgeoisie,* reduced the *parlement* and clergy to obedience, and won over the French nobles. Having by this policy strengthened his position in Paris, Mazarin was able still further to use his power in the interest of the peace of the kingdom and devote his attention to crushing all the resistance in the south, east, and west of France. Having accomplished the pacification of Provincial France, he was then in a position to turn with renewed vigour to the task of carrying out military operations against Spain and of bringing the war to a conclusion.

On learning that Mazarin had returned to France, the partisans of the princes in Provence met and re-solved to take up arms. The *parlement* of Aix, however, declared them rebels, and the Count of Alais, the governor, was arrested and imprisoned. In his place the Duke of Mercceur was appointed, and in May 1652 he was formally installed as governor of Provence. For upwards of a year Mercceur steadily pursued a consistent policy. Toulon, Tarascón, Sisteron, and Saint-Tropez resisted the royal authority and had to be reduced by force of arms. Other difficulties were rapidly settled owing to the good relations subsisting between Mercceur and the inhabitants, and by the end of 1653 Provence was pacified.

In Burgundy the difficulty was less. Épernon, who had succeeded Condé as governor, submitted, and Bellegarde, which was besieged in May 1653, yielded in June. In Guienne the state of things was far more serious than in any other part of France, and the resistance to the royal authority more determined. In Bordeaux princes and *parlement* and people were united in hatred of Mazarin. Democratic views were widely held, and, confident in their own powers of resistance, and buoyed up with hopes of foreign aid, the inhabitants prolonged the war till the end of July 1653. Condé, in undertaking in 1652 his famous journey to the Loire and then to Paris, had left the government of Bordeaux in the hands of his brother Conti, who was advised by a council which included the Duchess of Longueville, Marsin, and Lenet. Disorder soon broke out in Bordeaux. The *parlement* fell into two divisions—the minority known as the Little Fronde favouring moderate views; while the majority united with the extreme section of the people, known as the *Ormée* or *Ormistes*. Conti had the weakness to support an attack upon the moderate party of the *parlement* ; civil war ensued, and Bordeaux fell into the hands of the demagogues, whose actions recall those of the Jacobins in 1793-94. These internal dissensions favoured the progress of the royal arms. On the retirement of the Count of Harcourt from the command of the army, the Duke of Cándale, son of Épernon, was appointed. As soon as the royal authority was established in Paris, Mazarin took energetic measures to suppress the revolt in Guienne. The growth of a royalist party in Bordeaux was encouraged ; the Duke of Vendôme with a fleet appeared at the confluence of the rivers Garonne and Dordogne, and the Count of Daugnon, governor of Brouage, made terms. His defection was a fatal blow to the cause of the princes of Bordeaux. Attacked from within and without, the Ormée gradually realised that no help from either Spain or England was possible. Conti negotiated secretly with Mazarin, and at length a treaty was signed on July 31, 1653. The Dukes of Vendôme and Cándale entered Bordeaux; Marsin, Lenet, and other partisans of the princes were allowed to depart, and measures were taken to assure the tranquillity of Bordeaux. Only the leaders of the. Ormée were executed. Conti himself married one of Mazarin's gifted nieces, and the Duchess of Longueville, the evil genius of the house of Condé, made her peace with her husband, and on his death adopted a religious life in Paris. Mazarin was, however, not deceived by the appearances of loyalty in Bordeaux. He had rightly gauged the character of the inhabitants of the south-west of France, and knew that the treaty lately made had only " covered up the flame and not extinguished it." He ordered Vendôme and Cándale to take careful precautions against future outbreaks, and when a Spanish fleet appeared in November 1653, at the mouth of the Gironde, it met with no support.

Thus was concluded the long struggle of the Fronde. Over all France the royal authority had asserted itself. Internal disorder was rapidly disappearing before the almost complete extinction of Condé's faction as a power in the State. Henceforward the French nobles were no longer a danger to the State. They were employed in warfare or at the court, but had no opportunity of becoming great local magnates. Henceforward the *parlement* of Paris, shorn of its political functions, was forced to confine itself to its judicial duties, and to bow before the strong will of Louis XIV. Henceforward the principal government offices were filled by men who had sprung from the bourgeois class, or from that of the lesser nobles—men such as Colbert, Servien, Lionne, and le Tellier. Mazarin had successfully carried out and completed the work of Eichelieu. The great nobles had forfeited all claim to confidence. Their selfishness, incapacity, and want of patriotism had been fully illustrated during the period from 1648 to 1651, and Mazarin was fully justified in crushing for ever the last efforts to introduce feudalism into government. Having destroyed the two Frondes, and having re-established order and the authority of the king, Mazarin was called upon to give to the reorganised monarchy the force necessary to conquer its external foes. From 1653 to 1659 Mazarin successfully accomplished that task, and placed the French monarchy at the head of the nations of Europe. His first duty was to drive the Spaniards from Champagne, to attack them in Italy and Catalonia, to take from them the seaports of Flanders, and finally to compel them to make peace. It was not till the Peace of the Pyrenees was signed in 1659 that Mazarin's work was accomplished.

Throughout these years Mazarin had exhibited diplomatic qualities of a high order. Richelieu would probably at certain epochs have acted in a more decided manner. That at the end of 1650, after Rethel, Mazarin should have immediately adopted energetic measures to establish his position is incontestable. He ought also, after the campaign on the Loire, in 1652, to have taken Turenne's advice and advanced boldly on Paris and proclaimed Louis XIV. king. Instead of such decisive action, he preferred negotiations which caused the battle of Saint-Antoine and anarchy in Paris for some months. That Mazarin's position was peculiarly difficult is evident. Throughout these years the Spanish war proved of great assistance to Condé, and hampered the royal cause. Fortunately, Spain did not possess a general of special merit, and as soon as Turenne's period of treason ended all serious danger to France was over, though the loss of Dunkirk in September 1652 was sufficient evidence of the disastrous effects of Condé's rebellion. In addition to the Spanish alliance, the influence of French women upon the course of the civil wars added to Mazarin's responsibilities. The Duchess of Longueville was answerable in great part for the rising in Normandy in 1651, and for the treason of Turenne. She also threw all the weight of her influence on the side of rebellion when Condé at the time of the king's majority was still hesitating. She continued at Bordeaux to support Conti in 1653 in defying the royal power. Hardly less important was Madlle. de Montpensier, who took so notable a part in the battle of Saint-Antoine. The mother and wife of Condé both acted energetically against Mazarin, and the Duchess of Chevreuse was alternately his enemy and his ally. The influence of women during the period of the Frondes proved to be uniformly disastrous to the interests of France, and vastly increased Mazarin's difficulties. The memoirs of Madame de

Motteville and of de Retz teem with illustrations of the truth of this statement. Richelieu, it can hardly be doubted, would have long before 1648 suppressed the *parlement* and exiled his foes. Mazarin failed to foresee the seriousness of the storm which began to gather round him from the very moment of his accession to power ; and when the storm broke he

hesitated to take drastic measures. He believed in negotiations and diplomacy, and eventually his diplomacy succeeded. Though stern measures of repression would have brought the struggle to a speedy end, and saved France an infinity of suffering, it is impossible not to admire the resolution and perseverance shown by Mazarin. Time was on his side, and slowly but surely events turned out as he had anticipated. The reaction in favour of' the royal power steadily grew, and all the elements of disorder were one by one eliminated. He had continued the work of Eichelieu, and by the end of 1653 had arrived at the goal of the ambition of his predecessor. But he preferred devious paths to Richelieu's stern and rapid methods.

THE SPANISH WAR AND THE ENGLISH ALLIANCE

The continuance of internal trouble in France, and the death in November 1650 of William IL, Stadtholder of the United Provinces, upset all Mazarin's schemes with regard to Spain and England. The Peace of Münster, made in January 1648 between the Dutch and the Spaniards, had confounded his policy and frustrated all his hopes. But though his plans had for the moment failed, he trusted, by means of the influence of William II., to induce the States-General to cancel the peace. In that event he anticipated an early triumph over Spain, and an opportunity for interfering in England on behalf of the Stuarts. It seemed that the time had come to strike a blow against republican institutions and republican parties ; for while a republic had been established in England, the republican Fronde troubled France, and William II. 's republican opponents received encouragement from England. The New Fronde of the princes was on the side of Spain ; in England Spain was popular ; while the United Provinces had seceded from the French alliance and had joined Spain. Mazarin was therefore justified in considering the advisability of, uniting with William II. in attacking the Boman Catholic Netherlands, and in attempting the restoration of the Stuarts. The houses of Bourbon, Stuart, and Orange would thus join in opposition to the English Commonwealth, and a great blow would be inflicted on Spain. William IL's death on November 6, 1650, destroyed this scheme, and, like the Dutch alliance with Spain in 1648, came as an overwhelming blow to Mazarin's hopes. In December 1650 he had indeed, by the victory of RetheLT" driven the Spaniards out of Champagne, but his exile from France, and the general confusion which ensued, rendered any effective operations against the Spaniards in 1651 impossible. Moreover, Condé, who was supreme in Paris during the greater part of 1651, entered into negotiations with Spain, and was apparently prepared, in order to secure his own position, to make a definite alliance with Philip IV.

After the king had attained his majority in September 1651, Condé plunged into civil war, and had no hesitation in accepting the aid of the Spaniards. The Arch-duke Leopold without any difficulty retook Furnes and some other places, and in 1652 his troops won many successes. It was said by the Venetian minister that, while former years had been filled with constant victories for France, now every week brought the news of some loss. No decisive battle was fought, but the Spaniards gradually recaptured most of the places which France had won, at the expense of many lives and much treasure, in the earlier years of the war. In May 1652 they attacked and took Gravelines, which they had lost in 1644, and in August Dunkirk was closely invested and a regular siege of the place was begun. Recognising the advantages accruing to Spain from a continuance of the disorder in France, the archduke had decided not to send active help to Condé and his party, trusting that they would be strong enough to hold their own and continue the civil war. He therefore ordered Fuen-saldaña not to attack Paris in concert with the Duke of Lorraine in the summer of 1652, but to lead his army to Dunkirk.

Though Mazarin had long been aware of the danger which threatened Dunkirk, he failed to recognise the necessity of at once gaining the support of Oliver Cromwell. As early as 1650 he had noted the importance of England and the necessity of conciliating the English government, but it was not till later that events forced him to realise the necessity of an alliance. In June 1651 one of his own secretaries had been unable to enter Dunkirk owing to the presence of some twelve or fifteen English ships which were watching the town. Though, too, he was well aware that supplies and reinforcements could only be introduced by a fleet, he failed to recognise the strength of the anti-French feeling in England, and thus lost Dunkirk. The history of the loss of this important place illustrates admirably the methods of the cardinal, and the strength and weakness of his character. In 1651 he seems to have hoped to secure the aid of either the Dutch or the English fleet in order to save Dunkirk. Its governor Estrades, who in June 1651 advised Mazarin to collect all the troops then garrisoning towns in the north of France and to attack Paris, was helpless ; Dunkirk was besieged by the Spaniards and apparently could not hold out beyond the end of January 1652. To save the place secret negotiations had indeed been opened with England and Holland. With the latter power the French negotiations were opened probably at the close of November 1651; but owing to the protests of the Spanish ambassador, and to the dislike of the States to a fresh war, they had been broken off. Meanwhile Estrades had in all probability already offered to admit an English garrison into the town. Cromwell, with the assent of two members of the Council of State, had before this sent secretly a Colonel Fitzjames to Dunkirk, and the result of his mission was that Estrades seriously considered the possibility of delivering the town to the English government. In January 1652 Fitzjames was again sent to Dunkirk with definite overtures, which Cromwell intended to be presented to the French government. Estrades declared that the proposals of Cromwell were laid before Mazarin at Angers. At any rate, Mazarin was far from showing any anxiety to close the bargain. He was busy fighting Condé and his partisans on the Loire, and hoped that a decided success in that quarter would render the acceptance of the

English terms and the surrender of Dunkirk unnecessary. In April 1652 5000 English soldiers were assembled at Dover ready to be conveyed to Dunkirk. But Mazarin haggled and hesitated. He hoped that he could preserve Dunkirk by means of a relieving fleet, and that the English would not interfere with the French expedition. As Louis XIV.'s government still persisted in refusing to recognise the Commonwealth, Mazarin's hopes of English neutrality were destined to be disappointed, and a severe penalty was exacted for his failure to realise the true position of affairs.

Mazarin had indeed formed a plan, but none of the measures taken to relieve Dunkirk were of any avail. " God knows," he wrote to Estrades, " the trouble that I have taken during the last six months to send you help." There was only one way to relieve Dunkirk, and Mazarin only too late realised the vital importance to France of a friendly understanding with England. The JDuke of Vendôme, the French admiral, was ordered to bring a fleet from La Rochelle, and, taking advantage of the temporary absence of Blake and the English fleet, which was at that moment in pursuit of some Dutch ships, to throw supplies and reinforcements into Dunkirk. Vendôme, however, found the execution of his task beset with difficulties. Near the islands of Ré and Oléron he was attacked on August 19 by some Spanish ships and by some vessels under the Count of Daugnon, one of Condé's supporters. Though victorious, Vendôme had to put back into La Rochelle to refit and revictual. Delays occurred, and at last it was decided to collect ships from Picardy and Normandy, especially from Calais and Boulogne, and with them to assist the besieged garrison in Dunkirk. On September 14 this hastily equipped fleet, which numbered seven vessels and some fire-ships, set sail, and was met by some Spanish ships under the Marquis Of Leyde, who had surrendered Dunkirk to the French in 1646. Before a battle could take place, the English fleet of fifteen ships under Blake arrived and captured all the French vessels except one, which escaped under cover of the night. The following day, September 16, Dunkirk surrendered to the Spaniards. Mazarin's hesitation, and ignorance of the character of Cromwell, and of the true position of affairs in England, had brought upon France a great disaster. He had carried on his negotiations too long, fancying that by waiting he could obtain English neutrality at a much lower price. In April he seems to have almost made up his mind to hand over Dunkirk as the price of an English alliance against Spain. Had he done so France would have gained enormously, and the treaty of 1658 with England would have been antedated by some five years. But as yet he had not realised the tenacity of Cromwell and of his Council, and he hoped to gain his ends at a cheap rate. As it was, he overshot the mark, and the Italian diplomatist only learnt after bitter experience that methods suitable for dealing with continental statesmen were inadequate for treating with a man like Oliver Cromwell. He had, however, learnt his lesson, and in December 1652 the French government formally acknowledged the English Commonwealth.

Never was France in greater need of a powerful ally. The year 1652, which saw the fall of Dunkirk, to the great delight of Condé and his supporters, who boasted that they were now masters of the sea, saw also the loss of Cásale and Catalonia. The influence of France in Italy suffered a severe blow, and the Duke of Mantua, to whom was given the custody of Cásale, became the ally of Spain. In 1628 Cásale had been captured by Eichelieu, who also before his death had united Catalonia to the French crown. The loss of that great province was immediately due to the rebellion of Condé in 1651 and 1652. Marsin, the governor, was a supporter of the prince, and on the outbreak of the civil war had left Catalonia to aid in the revolt of Bordeaux. In 1653 it was Mazarin's duty to carry on the war with vigour against Spain, and to recover what had been lost since 1648.

For these extensive operations money was required, and Mazarin continued to find Fouquet's services in this respect invaluable. In December 1654 Mazarin divided the functions of the two superintendents. To Servien was given the department of expenditure, to Fouquet that of receipts. In other words, to Fouquet was allotted the whole management of loans. This division of functions was not made a moment too soon. Freed from the trammels imposed on him by his colleague, Fouquet proved equal to the demands made on him for the Spanish war. Though the king had no credit, the courteous Fouquet was regarded with confidence. He was known to be wealthy, he was easy of access, his manner was conciliatory, his financial abilities were undoubted. Men at once lent willingly to Fouquet, and Fouquet lent to the king. In 1656, after the capture of Valenciennes, Fouquet provided 900,000 livres ; at the end of 1657, 10,000,000 more.

Freed from immediate anxiety with regard to funds, Mazarin could devote himself to the overthrow of Spain. The recognition of the English Commonwealth, the dispersal of the discontented princes, and the suppression of rebellion in Guienne were valuable preliminary steps towards the attainment of this object. In 1653 Turenne defeated an attempt of Condé to capture Paris, and at the end of the year Sainte-Ménehould was taken. Though aided by her alliance with Condé, Spain could not resist the skill and energy of Turenne. In June 1654 Arras was captured, and in August Stenay was relieved. The success of the French was complete ; Condé and his allies were driven to Brussels, and the northern frontier was secure. Meanwhile Harcourt, who at a critical moment had thrown up his command in Guienne, and had hoped to establish himself as an independent prince in Alsace and Philipsburg, was compelled, through Mazarin's astuteness, to surrender his government; and the year 1654 ended in brilliant fashion by the capture of Quesnoi, Binche, and Clermont. The tide of Spanish successes had at last been checked, and Louis XIV., who had been crowned amid circumstances of great solemnity on June 7, 1654, had been himself present with the army besieging Stenay.

The relief of Arras was the turning-point in the history of the war. Arras had always been regarded as one of " the gems of the Spanish monarchy," and its capture by France marked the beginning of that revival of the French military power which developed with such amazing rapidity during the ensuing years of Louis XIV.'s reign.

As if to counterbalance these successes, certain events occurred about the same time which demonstrated the shifting character of Italian politics, and the necessity for firmness in dealing with any attempt to revive the animosities of the Fronde period. In Italy a fresh effort at intervention on the part of France ended in failure. The Duke of Guise had led an expedition to Naples, which, it was expected, would rise on the appearance of the French fleet. But the Spaniards met him with a superior armament, and Guise was compelled to return somewhat ignominiously to France. Equally annoying to Mazarin was the escape from Vincennes of the Cardinal de Retz. On the death of the Archbishop of Paris in March 1654, de Retz had succeeded to his position, but the government would not recognise the coadjutor's claim to the office. Before the end of the month de Retz, in hopes of securing his release, resigned his archbishopric, and was transferred to the castle of Nantes, where he was treated with leniency. His resignation was, however, not accepted by Pope Innocent X who hated Mazarin and was friendly to de Retz, on whom he had previously bestowed a cardinal's hat. On August 8 that worthy managed to escape to Spain, and at the same time sent to the government a revocation of his resignation as archbishop. In November 1654 he arrived in Rome, and was welcomed by the Pope. On January 7, 1655, Innocent X. died, to the great joy of the Roman populace, and it was at that moment that Lionne arrived at Rome with special instructions from Mazarin to secure a papal repudiation of the claims of de Retz. In spite of the efforts of the French party among the cardinals, Fabio Chigi, the Spanish candidate, was, on April 7, elected Pope as Alexander VII. The new Pope, who had taken part in the negotiations leading to the Peace of Westphalia, had shown an almost uniform hostility to France. Alexander at first appeared willing to give fair consideration to the case of de Retz. But he deferred appointing commissioners to consider the matter, and on June 2 he gave de Retz the pallium, thus recognising him as Archbishop of Paris. Fortified by this support, de Retz issued orders to certain of the clergy in

Paris, and handed over the administration of his diocese to two ecclesiastics, one of whom, Chassebras, who was in charge of the Madeleine, by his intrigues stirred up opposition to Mazarin. He became the centre of a cabal with which the *parlement* and all enemies of the minister sympathised. Mazarin spoke in severe terms of him in a letter to Lionne. "There is," he said, " no greater Jansenist than that self-styled grand vicar of de Retz. He does an extraordinary amount of harm ; moves heaven and earth to organise a cabal in Paris ; and carries out blindly every measure suggested to him by the adherents of de Retz." Thus, at the opening of the campaign of 1655 against Spain, Mazarin found himself hampered by de Retz's attempts to stir up sedition in Paris. It was necessary once for all to crush the intriguing archbishop, and Mazarin spared no trouble to ensure the success of Lionne's mission in Rome. The list of charges brought against de Retz was a heavy one. He had taken part in the civil war against the king, he had intrigued with the Spaniards and with Condé, he had striven to stir up the nobles of Brittany, and after his late flight to Nantes he had sent emissaries to engage in plots in Paris. In a word, the archbishop was charged with having stirred up rebellion and sedition, and with being an abandoned criminal. As he was also a Jansenist, it was hoped he would receive little consideration from the Pope. Alexander VII. was an enemy of the Jansenists, with whom Mazarin had as little sympathy as he had with any of the works undertaken by the Port Royalists, or with the doctrines inculcated in the *Augustinus.* The support received by de Retz from the Jansenists, however, drew the attention of the government to a struggle between the Jesuits and Jansenists which was mainly theological.

Mazarin's ministry coincided with a period of religious fervour which was indicated by the growth of monasteries, by the lives of such men as Saint Vincent de Paul, and by the foundation of Port Royal. Of this foundation the Abbé de St. Cyran was in 1634 placed in charge, and he then closely associated it with the new tenets of Jansenism. In 1640 the *Augustinus* — the great posthumous work of Cornelius Jansen—appeared, in which he inculcated St. Augustine's teaching on the doctrine of grace, and made an attempt to reform the Church. In 1653 the influence of the Jesuits secured the condemnation by Innocent X. of five propositions contained in the book. Though the Jansenists were forced to yield to the papal authority, numerous issues were raised by the *Augustinus* which led to long and bitter controversies. Mazarin, who was naturally inclined to toleration, had by his moderation allayed the fears of the Huguenots on Richelieu's death, with the result that they remained tranquil during the Fronde troubles. Though pressed to adopt a policy of persecution, he hoped to be equally successful in bringing to a peaceable close the agitation which had grown out of the Jansenist movement. In his policy of conciliation he was ably seconded by Arnauld d'Andilly, one of the chiefs of the Jansenist party, and for a time peace was assured. But before long quarrels again burst forth, for the majority of the Jansenists had not the moderation of Arnauld dAndilly. It was only natural that the court should view with suspicion the Jansenist movement. The princes in the Fronde struggle had shown a tendency towards Jansenism, and the Jansenists had espoused the cause of de Eetz. Thus the Jansenists received no support from the royal power, and remained politically insignificant. But from a theological point of view they had an importance which increased as time went on, and led to a long-continued struggle in the next century over the Bull Unigenitus. The Jansenists aimed," it has been said, " at a conservative restoration of the theology of the fourth century, and, resisting the papal claims and dogma of infallibility, fell back on the authority of councils." Thus, while their political tendencies were offensive to the court, their theological views brought them into collision with the Jesuits and the papacy. The Jansenists held and defended the stern views of Jansen as to the efficacy of grace and the inability of man to attain to perfection, and the members of Port Royal, whose cloister life was remarkable for purity and simplicity, were devotedly attached to Jansenist doctrines. In an evil moment for themselves the Jesuits attacked the inmates of Port Royal, and in their defence Pascal in 1656 published his famous *Provincial Letters.* Though unable to make any adequate reply to Pascal's accusations, the Jesuists were sufficiently influential to secure their condemnation at Rome, and in 1660 the *Provincial Letters* were publicly burnt in Paris. In 1660 and 1661 many schools which were controlled by Port Royal were closed, and throughout Louis XIV.'s reign Jansenism was barely tolerated. At the close of his life Louis fell under the influence of the Jesuits, and Port Royal was destroyed and its inmates banished. Mazarin's ministry thus saw the beginning of controversies which continued till the Revolution of 1789, but it must be remembered that Mazarin refused to destroy Port Royal and carry out a policy of extermination of the Jansenists, as was suggested to him. So strong, however, was the feeling on the part of the leading churchmen in favour of orthodoxy, that Mazarin showed no little wisdom in making the charge of Jansenism one of the principal points in his accusations against de Retz. Father Duneau, a Jesuit who was one of Mazarin's principal agents in Rome, had represented to Alexander VII. the danger of allowing de Retz, who favoured the Jansenists, to remain at the head of the Paris diocese. In July 1655, the papal confessor, Father Sforza Palavici freely to the Pope of the alliance between de Retz and the Jansenists. As not only de Retz but also many of his friends were Jansenists, Mazarin had good reason for expecting that the Pope would at once refuse to agree to the petition of the intriguing archbishop. But Alexander believed that de Retz had merely adopted Jansenism for political purposes, and declared that though de Retz might have taken money from the Jansenists, he had preached against the doctrines of Jansen. Lionne had already been sent as a special envoy to Rome, and he demanded that proceedings should be taken against de Retz. After innumerable delays Alexander appointed a commission to hear the charges against the Archbishop of Paris. But the conditions attached to the papal brief made it impossible for Mazarin to accept it. The Pope insisted that the *parlement* of Paris and the assembly of the clergy should sanction the proposed agreements (which included the appointment of a suffragan in place of de Retz), and Mazarin at once refused to allow any organisation in France to interfere with the supreme power of the king. The absolute and despotic power in France, he said, resided in the person of the king alone, and no organisation in the kingdom could share it. In writing to the queen he declared that to negotiate with the *parlement* or the assembly of the clergy would be derogatory to the power of the king, and would reduce Louis to the position of a doge of the republic of France.

Lionne was recalled in 1656 and the proceedings against de Retz were dropped. Alexander, however, did little to aid the archbishop, who eventually resigned his post, while the suffragan regarded himself as holding his office from Louis XIV. De Retz received several abbeys, and in 1665 visited Paris, where he was coldly received by Louis XIV. He was nevertheless employed on missions to Rome, and during his later years wrote his famous memoirs.

Equally drastic was Mazarin's treatment of the *parlement* of Paris, and equally emphatic was his assertion of the royal authority. Early in 1655 a *lit de justice* had registered an edict imposing taxes which were required for the Avar. Hearing that the *parlement* on April 13 was prepared to criticise the edict, Louis XIV., who was then hunting at Vincennes, hurried back to the Palais de Justica and forbade the continuance of the discussion. He and Mazarin were resolved that there should be no renewal of the Fronde, and any attempt of the *parlement* to adopt an independent tone was at once checked.

The campaign of 1655 was successful. The important town of Landrecies was taken, and Turenne, advancing between the Scheldt and the Sambre, compelled the capitulation of the towns of Condé and Saint-Guillain. Louis XIV. himself witnessed the success of his general, and with him almost reached the famous stronghold of Mons.

In other ways the year 1655 proved fortunate. The Spaniards had arrested and imprisoned the adventurous Duke of Lorraine at the beginning of 1654. At the close of 1655 the Lorraine army declared for France. In

Catalonia and Italy no events of importance took place, but the events of the year had clearly demonstrated the increasing power of France. In 1653 Mazarin had brought to an end the provincial Fronde; in 1654 the Spaniards had been driven from Champagne, and the .Duke of Lorraine had been won over by skilful diplomacy; in 1655 Turenne had penetrated into Hainault. It was now necessary to retake the maritime towns of Xxravelines, Mardyke, and Dunkirk. The death of William IL, Prince of Orange, in November 1650 had destroyed all chance of securing a Dutch alliance and the co-operation of the Dutch fleet, and Mazarin had, as we have seen, turned his attention to England. The action taken by Blake at the time of the Spanish conquest of Dunkirk had been followed by Antony of Bordeaux being in December 1652 formally accredited as the French envoy to the English government. But the relations between France and England remained unsettled. English merchantmen suffered from pirates fitted out in French seaports, and reprisals were frequent. The protection, too, given by France to Charles Stuart was a constant source of irritation to the English people, who were very suspicious of a government at the head of which was a cardinal. In the English Council there was a strong party which desired war with France, and which found a lever to work upon in Cromwell's Protestant sympathies and belief that the French Protestants were continually persecuted. Cromwell was resolved to help the Frèrich Protestants should they require assistance. The residence of the exiled Stuarts in France constituted in his opinion a danger to the Protectorate, and it was suspected that when once Mazarin had conquered Spain he would aid in the restoration of Charles Stuart, and so bring England into subservience to France.

In January 1654 Mazarin sent a special agent, the Baron de Baas, to assure Cromwell that, if England and France concluded an alliance, Charles Stuart should no longer be allowed to reside in France. The situation was for some time critical, and rarely had Mazarin's imperturbable temper, perseverance, and diplomatic skill been so tested. Lambert and the officers clamoured for a French war, and the Archduke Leopold authorised Cardenas, the Spanish envoy, to offer the English government £120,000 a year. Mazarin, who had already authorised Bordeaux to recognise the Protectorate, instructed Baas to offer the same amount, and to point out that Spain was unable to pay the proffered sum. The Dutch war being concluded, an alliance with Spain was looked for in England. Cardenas had now offered £300,000 a year, and Cromwell had accepted the offer, though he agreed to accept £100,000 for the time being, the rest to be paid later. But the government of the Low Countries was unable to raise that money, and the relations between England and Spain quickly became strained. England was bent on an attack on the West Indies; and the relief of Arras by Turenne in August 1654 demonstrated to Cromwell that Spain was on the losing side. Mazarin at the same time convinced him that the danger to the Protestants was imaginary, and Cromwell at once began to regard the expedition to the Spanish West Indies as an attack on the Pope and the Inquisition. Before, however, an alliance between France and England was made, the massacre of the Yaudois in January 1655 took place. Amid circumstances of intense cruelty the Duke of Savoy expelled the Protestant Vaudois from their valleys. Cromwell's vigorous remonstrances, and his intimation that no treaty with France would be signed till restitution had been made to the Vaudois, quickened Mazarin's action. The Duke of Savoy was ordered to restore the privileges of the Vaudois, and to cause all persecution to cease. In August 1655 Mazarin's tolerant policy was accepted and acted upon by the Duke of Savoy, while England's position in Europe had been strengthened by Cromwell's successful intervention.

On November 3, 1655, the Treaty of Westminster I between France and England was signed, and Spain's remaining chance of success in her struggle with Louis XIV. disappeared. By this treaty the commercial relations between France and England were regulated. Charles Stuart apd his brother were to leave France, all acts of piracy were to cease, and various restrictions on trade were removed. England at once declared war upon Spain, and it was obvious that Philip IV. could i not hope to contend successfully against France, England, and Portugal. Mazarin had won a remarkable diplomatic triumph. His policy was similar to that employed, at other periods of his career. He decided on the goaf which was to be reached, on the object to be attained. But though his aims were statesmanlike, and in full agreement with what Richelieu would have advocated, Mazarin's methods were peculiar to himself. Always ready to negotiate, and resolved to take no offence, he was not infrequently placed in an undignified position. In the pursuit of what he desired Mazarin too often cast aside dignity, humbled himself before his adversaries, though in the end he carried his point. The difficulties in his negotiations with Cromwell were immense, and the obstacles to an alliance innumerable. Mazarin, however, steadily pursued his object, England did not make a Spanish alliance, and France, though temporarily losing Dunkirk, concluded the triumphant Peace of the Pyrenees.

After the Treaty of Westminster had been signed, Lionne was sent secretly to Spain to begin negotiations for peace. But all chances of an immediate settlement were destroyed by the unexpected successes won by Condé in the campaign of 1656. Turenne had besieged Valenciennes, which on July 15 was relieved by Condé, a division of the French army under the incapable la Ferté Senneterre being almost annihilated. The town of Condé was taken from the French, who were in danger of losing the advantages of the late campaigns. Vigorous measures were required at home to lessen the existing misery ; abroad, to bring the war to a conclusion. In January 1656 the *parlement* of Paris had protested against the depreciation of the coinage, and had been supported by the *parlements* of Toulouse and Grenoble. The *parlement* continued its remonstrances, and several of its members were banished. Eventually a compromise was arranged, and peace was restored. But the action of the *parlement* was only symptomatic of the general feeling of unrest in the country, where peasant risings were becoming frequent.

The disaster at Valenciennes and the unrest in France combined to render Mazarin anxious to unite more closely with England, and Cromwell, aware that Spain was about to assist Charles Stuart, was equally ready to draw nearer France. On March 28, 1657, an offensive and defensive treaty was signed at Paris. The object of this Treaty of Paris was to force Spain to make peace. The two powers were to undertake the sieges of Gravelines and Dunkirk by sea and by land. At the same time Cromwell engaged to tolerate Roman Catholicism in all places in Flanders which were handed over to England, and undertook to keep possession of Dunkirk only. Such were the principal terms of this famous treaty, which was fraught with far-reaching results for Europe, and which had such immediate and important effects upon the course of the war between France and Spain. The English alliance was one of the master strokes of Mazarin's policy, and its wisdom was fully justified.

CARDINAL MAZARIN

THE LEAGUE OF THE RHINE AND THE PEACE OF THE PYRENEES

The Treaty of Paris was not made a month too soon, for the campaign opened disastrously for France. The Spaniards captured Saint-Guillain in March, and in June Condé forced Turenne to abandon the siege of Cambray. But after these failures success attended the arms of the French and English. Don John of Austria, who commanded the Spanish troops, was incapable ; Montmédy capitulated to the French in August ; and Turenne not only captured Saint-Venant, but compelled the Spaniards to raise the siege of Ardres. Meanwhile, Louis XIY. had reviewed the English forces at Montreuil, and after a siege of four days Mardyke surrendered on October 3 to Turenne, who handed it over to his English allies. This success strengthened the good relations existing between Mazarin ancl Cromwell, though the cession of Mardyke to England called forth loud protestations from those who disliked the English alliance. At the same time complaints were made in England that Dunkirk had not been captured. Mazarin pointed out to Bordeaux that the English forces had arrived late, and that Spain had thrown reinforcements into Dunkirk and Gravelines. He urged that more English troops should be sent to defend Mardyke from the attacks of the Spanish forces. Till the following summer the combined English and French armies worked hard in strengthening their position, preparatory to an onslaught on Dunkirk.

Meanwhile, Mazarin was busy at Metz in conducting some delicate negotiations. The Emperor Ferdinand III. had died on April 1, 1657. In spite of the terms of the Peace of Westphalia, he had constantly assisted the Spaniards, and Mazarin had frequently protested against his violations of the treaty. In August

1656 Mazarin wrote to de Gravel, the French representative at Mainz, that the Emperor had not only supplied Spain with troops, but had lately resolved to send into Italy some 10,000 men to attack the Duke of Modena, the ally of France. Mazarin further remarked that the Emperor's conduct was due to the influence of the Spaniards. In 1649 Philip IV., King of Spain, had married Maria-Anna of Austria, daughter of Ferdinand.

"In consequence of this marriage," said Mazarin, "the Spaniards think they are masters of the imperial court, and therefore of all Germany." "These facts," he continued, " should open the eyes of the electors and of all German princes, and show them the necessity of opposing without delay attempts to subject them to Spanish domination." Consequently, on Ferdinand III.'s death the electors resolved to shake themselves free from the influence of the house of Hapsburg. Leopold, son of Ferdinand, had already been proclaimed King of Hungary, and it was necessary to combat his pretensions to the imperial throne. Mazarin even ordered Bordeaux to urge Cromwell to assist him in his policy, and pointed out that Leopold had ratified his father's engagements to support Casimir, the Roman Catholic king of Poland, against Charles X., king of Sweden and England's ally.

Not content with attempting to stir up England and Sweden to oppose the candidature of Leopold, Mazarin, accompanied by Louis XIV., spent the months of September and October 1657 at Metz, engaged in negotiations with the electors. Already the German princes had shown that they did not consider that the welfare and independence of the secondary states in Germany were sufficiently guaranteed by the Peace of Westphalia. In 1651 the three ecclesiastical electors, together with the Elector of Bavaria, the Bishop of Münster, the Count Palatine, and the Dukes of Neuburg and Juliers, had formed a League of the Rhine for the defence of their common interests. On their side the Protestant princes had also formed a League, which included the King of Sweden, the Dukes of Brunswick, Limburg, Zell, Wolfenbüttel, and Hanover, and the

Landgrave of Hesse-Cassel. Thus Germany was prepared for the diplomatic overtures of Mazarin, and ready to take steps to maintain the Peace of Westphalia.

Though suffering from gout, Mazarin showed the greatest activity. He carried on numerous sets of negotiations, and at ihe same time instructed Louis XIV. in the political condition of Europe, and explained to him the character of the interests of the various powers. Never had Mazarin's diplomacy been more active, never during his ministry had his hopes seemed more sure of fulfilment than at the close of 1657. Montmédy, Saint-Venant, and Mardyke had been taken from Spain, the English were co-operating with their French allies in capturing the maritime towns of Flanders, the Spanish influence at Vienna was destroyed. It remained for him to check permanently the power of the Emperor, and with the aid of England finally to crush Spain. The first of these tasks was accomplished in August 1658, when Lionne successfully united the two German leagues in the League of the Rhine, under the auspices of France. Mazarin had hoped to secure the election of a prince who did not belong to the Hapsburg house. The Duke of Neuburg, the Elector of Bavaria, and even Louis XIV. seem to have suggested themselves to his mind at different times. The Duke of Neuburg, however, did not prove a popular candidate, and the Elector of Bavaria was a weak prince devoted to the Hapsburgs. Gradually it became clear to Mazarin that the influence of tradition and an expectation of future favours by the electors tended to favour the choice of Leopold. Mazarin had little difficulty in changing his front. He declared that

Louis XIV. had never aspired to the Empire, and he devoted his energies to so limiting the power of the new Emperor that he would be unable to help the Spaniards in their war against France.

On July 18 Leopold having accepted certain conditions imposed upon him by the electors, was elected Emperor. He swore to observe scrupulously the conditions of the Peace of Westphalia and not to interfere in the war between France and Spain. Before, however, the League of the Rhine was formed, the young and warlike King of Sweden proposed to plunge into a war with the Emperor. Such a course of action, leading to general confusion in Germany, and probably to French intervention, would have been conducive to the advantage of Spain, and fatal to Mazarin's plans for narrowing down the struggle into one between Spain on the one hand and England and France on the other. The best means to defeat this project was to make a league among the German princes for the preservation of their independence. Charles X. yielded to the pacific advice of Mazarin, and on August 14, 1658, was formed the League of the Rhine, which was joined by the King of Sweden, six of the electors, and other German princes. On the next day Louis XIV. joined the League, engaging with the other members to defend the settlement of the Peace of Westphalia. The signatories agreed to force, if necessary, the Emperor to carry out the promises made at his election. Mazarin had won a fresh diplomatic victory, and after events fully justified his efforts and the vast sums expended in bribery. According to Mazarin he temporarily ruined himself in buying the smaller German princes. For many years, however, French influence was preponderant in Germany, and Louis XIV.'s position in Europe was largely due to Mazarin's formation of the League of the Rhine.In uniting the German Protestant and Roman Catholic princes of Germany in the League of the Rhine, Mazarin had successfully affirmed the principles of toleration which he himself held, and which had been proclaimed in the Peace of Westphalia. He had, too, placed the Empire under a further obligation to France by saving it from the war which the kings of Sweden and Spain wished to stir up within it. He had carried out the policy of Richelieu towards Germany, and by his prudence and moderation had gained for France the gratitude of the German people. It was not till Louis XIV. allowed himself to be carried away by overweening ambition, and to attack Germany by his Chambers of Reunion, that the Empire united with the Emperor in resisting a policy which ran directly counter to that adopted by Richelieu and Mazarin. During Mazarin's successful diplomacy in Germany, a fresh blow was being struck at thefepanish Bourbons. On March 28, 1658, a new treaty had been signed with Cromwell, and it was again distinctly laid down that the allied French and English forces were to combine for the conquest of Gravelines and Dunkirk. The campaign opened badly for France. Hesdin through treachery fell into the hands of the Spaniards ; and owing to his rashness and imprudence the Marshal d'Aumont was defeated in an attempt to seize Ostend, and was himself taken prisoner. Mazarin, however, was by no means discouraged. With the king and Anne of Austria he proceeded to Calais, and pressed on the preparations for the siege of Dunkirk. The difficulties were immense. The Spaniards heldBergues, Fumes, Nieuport, and Gravelines, and were resolved to defend Dunkirk to the last. At the end of May the court moved to Mardyke, so as to be nearer to the scene of operations, and Louis XIV. interested himself in providing for the welfare of the soldiers. On June 14 the allied forces won the battle of the Dunes, aud on the 23rd instant Dunkirk capitulated and was handed over to the English. Though

Spain had suffered a severe disaster, Mazarin was violently attacked for carrying out the treaty with England and surrendering Dunkirk. In vain did Mazarin point out that had England and Spain united, the French cause would have seriously suffered, and that the alliances of Louis XIV. with Sweden and Holland had proved insufficient for the overthrow of the Hapsburgs. Public opinion, however, moderated itself before the succession of victories gained by Turenne. That master of the art of warfare had seized Bergues, Furnes, and Dixmude in July, and in August 27 Gravelines capitulated. In the meantime Louis XIV. had fallen so seriously ill at Mardyke that his life was despaired of, and cabals were formed for the overthrow of Mazarin. The cardinal, however, was well informed as to the existence and character of the plots, and exiled the conspirators. The king recovered, but on September 3 Oliver Cromwell died. He had proved an invaluable friend to France, and England had gained enormously from the war with Spain. The alliance between the two countries continued during Richard Cromwell's government, and the new Protector, in view of the numerous factions which existed in England, had every reason to adhere to the treaty with France. Meanwhile, the autumn brought fresh triumphs to the government of Louis XIV. On September 9 Turenne had invaded Flanders and taken Oudenarde. Leaving Don John of Austria in Brussels and Condé in Tournay, Turenne retired to the Lys, and occupied Menin and Ypres. The chateau of Commines on the Lys next fell, and Turenne busied himself in fortifying the conquered places.

The year 1658 had proved disastrous to Spain. She had been defeated in Flanders by the French and in the province of Alen te jo by the Portuguese. Her position in the Milanese was threatened, and the English overcame her fleets at sea. Peace was absolutely necessary ; but the pride of Philip IV. stood in the way of any settlement. To force the Spanish king to come to terms, and to induce him to consent to the marriage of the Infanta and Louis XIV., Mazarin had recourse to an artifice. He made formal proposals for the marriage of Margaret of Savoy with the young king, and with the court proceeded in October 1658 to Lyons, in order to meet the Duchess of Savoy and her daughter. The success of his plans was, however, for a time endangered by the infatuation of Louis for Maria Mancini, one of Mazarin's nieces. Anne of Austria, who had set her heart on the Spanish match, was in despair. The event bore high testimony to

Mazarin's foresight, firmness, and diplomatic skill. On November 28, 1658, the Duchess of Savoy and her daughter arrived at Lyons, and almost simultaneously Antonio Pimentelli, a Spanish envoy, brought proposals for peace and the offer of the hand of the Infanta. On December 8 the Savoyard princesses left Lyons, and shortly afterwards serious negotiations with Spain were begun. On no previous occasion were Mazarin's diplomatic talents more necessary. Philip IV. and his ministers still hoped that fortune would declare itself on the side of Spain, and had a vague belief that the Emperor Leopold would break the Peace of Westphalia and the promises made on his election, and come to the assistance of the Spanish Bourbons.

Having acquainted Richard Cromwell and the French allies in Germany of the Spanish proposals, conferences were opened near Paris early in 1659. In May a suspension of arms was arranged ; during the greater part of the year negotiations proceeded. Meanwhile, Louis XIV.'s attachment for Maria Mancini had increased, and it was only by the exercise of patience and firmness that Mazarin secured obedience to his wishes. After the middle of August Louis' passion for Maria subsided, and he turned his attention to the peace negotiations. Peace was indeed the sincere wish of Mazarin. The war with Spain had lasted since1635, and had wrought havoc in the north-east of France. The country had been cruelly devastated ; churches without number had been destroyed. In 1657 and 1658 famine and flood had added a new horror to the calamities of war. Troyes, Chalons, Rheims, and many other places suffered from inundations, and the Seine in February 1658 was full of wreckage. Bossuet, preaching at Metz in 1658, gave eloquent expression to the desire for peace, which was shared with Mazarin by all classes in France. On June 4, 1659, a treaty was signed, the principal terms of the final arrangements between France and Spain were arranged, and it was decided that the many questions which required adjustment and

settlement should be discussed on the Isle of Pheasants, situated in the river Bidassoa, between Mazarin and Don Luis de Haro. At these conferences, which took place between August and November, appeared envoys from England, Rome, Sweden, Germany, Savoy, Modena, and Lorraine. Mazarin had, moreover, to listen to complaints from the envoys of the King of Sweden, and of the electors of Mainz and Cologne, against the Emperor Leopold, who, in consequence of the northern war, had sent troops into Pomerania. An additional reason was thus forced upon Mazarin for the immediate conclusion of peace, in order to enable him to deal with the complicated affairs of Northern Europe, where Charles X. was pursuing his meteoric career, and to compel the Emperor to respect the Peace of Westphalia and the terms of the capitulation which he had agreed to on his accession. On November 7, 1659, the Peace of the Pyrenees was signed, and a fitting end was brought to Mazarin's efforts. By this peace France obtained Roussillon, Conflans, Artois, except Aire and Saint-Omer, and portions of Luxemburg, Hainault, and Flanders. France was confirmed in her possession of Alsace, retained Pinerolo, and though on certain terms the Duke of Lorraine was to be reinstated in his dominions, the fortifications of Nancy were to be destroyed, and Louis XIV. secured the duchy of Bar, the county of Clermont, Stenay, Dun, Jametz, and Moyenvic. An easy entry for French armies in the future into Lorraine, Flanders, Hainault, and Luxemburg was thus assured. Great difficulty was experienced with regard to Condé. The Spanish minister had asked that the prince should be restored to his former governments, but Mazarin firmly refused to give any indulgence to a traitor, or to permit Condé to enjoy a position in which he could again be a menace to the monarchy. Eventually it was settled that on condition (1) that Spain ceded Avesnes and gave Juliers to the Duke of Neuburg, one of the allies of France ; and (2) that Condé asked pardon of the King of France, he should receive his private estate, and be made governor of Burgundy and Bresse. To these terms Condé agreed, and became one of Louis' most submissive courtiers. Portugal was not included in the treaty, though France obtained an amnesty for the Catalans and Neapolitans who had sided with her.

Though the treaty of June 4 had provided for the marriage of Louis XIV. with the Infanta, the terms of the arrangement were again fully discussed,Don Luis de Haro insisting that the princess should renounce her rights to the Spanish succession. Eventually Mazarin agreed to the renunciation, on condition that she received a dowry of 500,000 crowns, payable in three years. The articles of the marriage treaty were so drawn by Lionne that, if the money were not paid within the allotted time, the renunciation became null and void. The affairs of England were also discussed, and Charles II., who was present, endeavoured to secure the aid of France and

Spain in effecting his restoration. Both Mazarin and Don Luis were in favour of the Stuart restoration, but Mazarin refused to take any part in the war between England and Spain, or to espouse the cause of Charles II.

Peace was now made, and France had established her superiority over Spain. The great work of Mazarin was finished and the policy of Henry IV. and Richelieu was justified. Turenne, Fouquet, and others, however, were dissatisfied with the conclusion of peace, and were of opinion that the continuance of the war would have been advantageous to France. It was urged that Spain was so weakened that the conquest of the whole of the Spanish Netherlands could easily have been effected, and the Spanish monarchy dismembered. Mazarin, however, was right in concluding peace. France was exhausted, her finances in confusion, her people anxious for the end of hostilities. England, distracted by internal troubles, was no longer an effective ally; and had France persevered in her attempts to secure the Spanish Netherlands, she would probably have brought upon herself the active opposition of Holland and the Emperor. Mazarin, too, was anxious to bring French influence to bear upon the combatants in the Baltic and to end the northern war. It was also necessary to examine more closely into the condition of the finances and into Fouquet's administration.

One of the articles in the Treaty of the Pyrenees had contemplated the intervention of France or Spain as mediators in the northern war. Don Luis de Haro, however, showed no inclination to take any part in the work of mediation, and it was left to Mazarin to re-establish peace in the Baltic. France was indeed deeply interested in the work of pacification. Several of the allies of Louis XIV. were engaged in the war, and the Emperor had already taken part and violated the Treaty of Westphalia. Servien strongly urged that help should be given to Sweden, the ancient ally of France, and a valuable counterpoise to the power of the Emperor in Germany.

The northern war had begun in 1655 by the invasion of Poland by Charles X. of Sweden. John Casimir, King of Poland, who had married Marie de Gonzague-Nevers, a French princess, lost the greater part of his kingdom, and Warsaw fell. Disregarding Mazarin's counsels of prudence and moderation, Charles X. attacked and made an enemy of Frederick William, Elector of Brandenburg ; while the Poles, taking advantage of this diversion, drove the Swedes out of their territory. Charles at once threw himself on Poland, and after the famous three days' battle of Warsaw (July 28, 29, 30, 1656), again conquered the country. Alarmed at the rapid success of Sweden, a coalition, including Russia, Poland, Brandenburg, and Denmark, was formed in 1657. Leopold of Austria, then King of Hungary, also allied himself with Poland and sent troops, while Holland was prepared to oppose the conversion of the Baltic into a Swedish lake. Menaced by this formidable league, Charles attacked Denmark and besieged Copenhagen. Unable to offer any adequate resistance, the Danes willingly accepted the mediation of France and England, and on February 28, 1658, made the Treaty of Roskild, by which Sweden secured several provinces. War again broke out in the summer between Denmark and Sweden, and in August Copenhagen was a second time besieged. The projects of Charles X. inctoded the annexation of Denmark and Norway to Sweden, and the occupation of Courland, Pilau, and Dantzig. He. would thus dominate the Baltic and rule over a powerful northern empire. Holland at once took alarm, defeated the Swedish fleet, and raised the siege of Copenhagen ; while a new coalition was formed, including Russia,

Poland, Brandenburg, Denmark, and Holland. The Emperor Leopold encouraged the allies and sent them reinforcements.

Such was the situation in the north during the summer of 1658. Charles X. had ignored his allies, and his rashness had tended to alienate both France and England. But Oliver Cromwell was always guided in his policy to Sweden by the conviction that the Roman Catholic governments had entered upon a conspiracy against all Protestant states. He was also keenly alive to the importance of safeguarding English trade. Consequently Cromwell was easily convinced by Mazarin of the necessity of preserving the balance of power in the Baltic. Mazarin definitely proposed that France and England should unite to bring about peace between Sweden and Denmark, and between Sweden and the rest of the coalition. Cromwell at once sent a fleet into the Baltic to oppose Dutch attempts at aggrandisement. Unable to resist France and England, Holland joined them in urging peace upon Sweden and Denmark. During 1659 Mazarin never ceased his pacific endeavours, and almost simultaneously with the meeting of Mazarin and Don Luis de Haro a peace congress was opened at Oliva under the presidency of Antoine de

Lumbres, the French ambassador in Poland. The proceedings were carried on slowly. The King of Sweden was ungrateful for the help given him by England and France, and obstinately refused to relinquish his schemes, while the Emperor was secretly doing all in his power to prolong the struggle and to drive the Swedes from their possessions in Germany. Imperial troops besieged Stettin, though in, doing so they acted contrary to the terms of the Peace of Westphalia. No sooner was the Peace of the Pyrenees signed than Mazarin interfered energetically on behalf of Sweden. Various circumstances enabled him to bring matters to a successful issue. Spain refused to give any assistance to the Emperor, and the members of the League of the Rhine were stirred up by de Gravel, the French envoy, to protest against the Emperor's attack on the King of Sweden, who, as Duke of Bremen and Verden, was a member of the Confederation. Mazarin himself declared that if the Emperor's attacks on Pomerania were continued France would send her armies to the assistance of Charles X. It is impossible to assert that Mazarin's efforts to bring about peace would have proved successful had not Charles X. died in March 1660. Obstinate, ambitious, and full of wild schemes of conquest, Charles X. had nothing in common with Mazarin, whose advice he usually treated with contempt. His death at this crisis facilitated the conclusion of peace. The negotiations at Oliva were complicated by the fact that the Queen of Poland was a French princess who complained of the partiality shown by Mazarin for Sweden. Both Sweden and Poland were the traditional allies of France, and it was a difficult matter to arrange a satisfactory settlement. Mazarin's skill proved, however, adequate for the task, and on May 3, 1660, the Treaty of Oliva was signed. John Casimir renounced all claim to the Swedish throne. Livonia was divided between Sweden and Poland, and the latter state received back Courland, Polish Prussia, and all towns in Pomerania lately occupied by the troops of the Elector of Brandenburg and the Emperor. This peace secured the independence of Prussia under the Great Elector, whose power was thereby greatly strengthened. On June 6, 1660, the Treaty of Copenhagen between Sweden and Denmark was concluded under the mediation of France, England, and Holland. Sweden gave up her recent conquests, but kept the provinces of Aland, Bleckingie, and Scania. Mazarin's diplomacy had again been successfully asserted. While Sweden, the ally of France, still preserved her superiority in the Baltic, Denmark, Poland, and Brandenburg had accepted the mediation of the government of Louis XIV. The pacification of the north did infinite credit to the patience, perseverance, and sagacity of the cardinal.

The same year that saw the conclusion of the Peace of Oliva witnessed the departure of a French expedition to aid Venice in her war against Turkey, and to repress piracy in the Barbary States. The French ambassador at Constantinople had been insulted by the Turks in 1658, and without declaring war upon The Porte, Mazarin decided to avenge the insult by aiding the Venetians in their defence of Candia. The expedition proved a failure, and it was not till a few years later that French troops accomplished the end aimed at by Mazarin by aiding the Imperialists to defeat the Turks in the battle of St. Gottland.

Mazarin's last negotiations were successfully carried out, and proved beneficial to France. By a treaty signed on December 16, 1660, Ferdinand Charles, Archduke of Austria, on condition of receiving a large sum of money, renounced all pretensions to Alsace and the Sungau (of which Altkirch was the capital), and it was at the same time settled that the county of Ferrette should also be ceded to France. In this satisfactory manner Mazarin succeeded in carrying out the stipulations of a clause in the Peace of Westphalia of the greatest interest and importance to France. On February 28, 1661, a few days before his death, Mazarin concluded a treaty with Charles IV, the Duke of Lorraine. The terms settled in the Peace of the Pyrenees were modified, and Charles IY. was re-established in his duchy, though in close dependence upon France.

While engaged on these negotiations with the northern powers, with Turkey, with the Archduke Ferdinand Charles, and with the Duke of Lorraine, Mazarin had also been occupied in the south of France. There the court remained all through the winter of 1659-60, and during its sojourn at Toulouse several interesting events occurred. Mazarin secured for himself from the Duke of Mantua the duchy of Nevers, and at the same time gave the Count of Harcourt the province of Anjou in place of the government of Alsace, which he kept in his own hands. He also endeavoured to deal with the finances of the kingdom. Fouquet, the superintendent, had been denounced by Colbert and by Hervart, who had examined the accounts. Since Servien's death in

February 1659, Fouquet's schemes had been unchecked. He spent immense sums upon the building of his château of Vaux-le-Vicomte, he employed spies to report to him the words of Mazarin and the king, he evidently wished to become the First Minister. The purchase and fortification of Belle-Isle seemed to presage a struggle between the magnificent Fouquet and the royal power. Fouquet's influence was undoubtedly considerable. *Procureur-général* as well as superintendent of the finances, Fouquet had not only amassed a large fortune, but had obtained for his relations and friends high positions in the church, the army, and the court. Liberal to extravagance, a patron of men of letters and artists, Fouquet had numerous friends in positions of trust. His power, wealth, and influence made him a dangerous man, and there is little doubt that he was prepared if necessary to stir up civil war. He had been useful during the years of stress, but he belonged to an order of things that was passing away. He had nothing in common with the views and position of such men as le Tellier, Servien, and Colbert. The future was with middle-class officialdom, with bureaucracy, and with centralisation. Fouquet wished to be the mayor of the palace. Mazarin was well aware of the advisability of ridding the government of Fouquet. In a memoir drawn up in October 1659 Colbert had painted Fouquet's faulty methods in the blackest colours, and had suggested sweeping reforms. But the principal obstacle to drastic financial reforms lay in the danger of shaking the credit of the government. The fall of Fouquet would increase the difficulty of obtaining money. This consideration may have decided Mazarin not to attack Fouquet. At any rate he had several interviews with the superintendent, and remained on good terms with him till his own death. It was left to Louis XIV. to carry out the suggestions of Colbert and to overthrow Fouquet and his system. Monsieur Chéruel, in his work, on Mazarin's ministry, says that Nicholas Fouquet was with his brother the evil genius of Mazarin, and blames the cardinal for not acting energetically upon Colbert's advice.

During the winter and spring of 1660 the court remained in the south of France. The Fronde had been strongly supported in some of the southern districts, and the Duke of Mercceur, who had succeeded the Count of Alais as governor of Provence, had been compelled to use force in order to quell the sedition at Toulouse. Mazarin hoped that the presence of the king would allay all discontent and promote a feeling of loyalty ; he was also anxious to improve the condition of the navy in the Mediterranean, and with that object visited in company with Louis XIV. the important town of Toulon. At Aix in Provence Louis had received the submission of Condé, and on February 3 the ratification of the Treaty of the Pyrenees. Later in the month he and the cardinal stayed at Toulon, and on March 2 he entered Marseilles. As in the case of Toulouse, Mercceur had been compelled to have recourse to arms before he could secure the submission of the citizens. An expedition was about the same time sent to compel the governor of the town of Orange, which belonged to the house of Orange-Nassau, to recognise the suzerainty of the King of France and to open its gates to his representative. From Marseilles the court proceeded to Avignon, Montpellier, and finally to Saint-Jean-de-Luz, where in June the marriage of Louis and the Infanta was celebrated. For the first time for many years Anne of Austria and her brother, Philip IV. of Spain, met on the Isle of Pheasants, and two days later, on June 6, the two kings had an. interview. Louis XIV. with his queen and court then returned to Fontainebleau, arriving on July 13. The state entry into Paris was not made till August 26, and was the occasion of great rejoicings. In the procession Mazarin's suite was equal to the royal household in magnificence.

First came seventy-two baggage mules, divided into three troops, and each troop adorned with embroidered silk and tapestry, the last troop clothed with coverings of scarlet velvet, on which were blazoned the cardinal's arms. Then followed twenty-four pages in rich liveries and on horseback, led by Mazarin's equerries, the Sieurs Fontenelle and Moreau. "Next came twelve Spanish jennets, accoutred in crimson embroidered velvet, and each led by two grooms. To these succeeded his carriages, seven in number, each drawn by six horses. The cardinal's private carriage was completely covered with goldsmith's work in silver gilt, and was surrounded by forty running footmen richly dressed, behind whom marched the Sieur de Besmo of Mazarin's body-guard." Mazarin, with Turenne, viewed the procession from a balcony, being too ill himself to take part in it. English affairs were during these celebrations engaging his attention, and demanded the exercise of all his diplomatic skill.

Before, however, the court had returned to Fontainebleau, the Restoration had taken place in England, and it seemed likely to be followed by a breach of the Anglo-French alliance. For some months Mazarin had been occupied with the consideration of the political situation in England. What was the true policy for France to adopt during the latter days of the weak rule of Richard Cromwell? The Treaty of Paris, made by Mazarin with Oliver Cromwell, had proved invaluable, but in accordance with the demands of the Protector, Charles II. had been forced to retire from France, while his mother, Henrietta Maria, remained, and had become a *persona grata* at the French court. While she looked forward to returning to England and to directing the policy of the restored monarchy, Charles II, Hyde, and the rest of his exiled friends held bitter feelings with regard to their treatment by the French government. In the early months of 1660, during his journeys through Languedoc and Provence, Mazarin was compelled to watch very carefully the various revolutionary phases through which England was passing, and to decide on the policy which France should adopt. A monarchical restoration in England was the ardent wish of Louis XIV. and his court, but any overt action in favour of Charles II. would rally all the antimonarchical sections in England and ruin Charles II.'s prospects. At the same time, Mazarin wished, in view of the possibility of a restoration, to stand well with Charles, and in some measure to remove the feelings of hostility which that prince felt towards France as the ally of the Commonwealth. It was quite evident to Mazarin that the continuance of anarchy in England would disgust all lovers of order and contribute to a restoration; it was equally evident that the interests of Charles II would be best served by inaction on the part of France. Mazarin recognised that Monk held the key of the position. While that general was deciding on his future action, Mazarin sent secretly to Charles II, who was then in Brussels, 100,000 crowns, and a promise of aid from France towards his restoration. The gravity of this blunder was at once apparent. Charles was doubtless shadowed by spies, but M. Chéruel charges Hyde and Ormond with having divulged Mazarin's intentions. In any case, Charles II.'s cause was for the time weakened, and general resentment prevailed in England at the notion of receiving a king through the agency of France. To destroy the evil effects of the publication of Mazarin's somewhat indiscreet action, Monk and the supporters of a restoration decided that Charles II. should reside in a country not dependent upon either France or Spain. Consequently the Prince proceeded to Breda, and on

May 8, 1660, was offered the English Crown by the Parliament.

For some months after the Restoration France and England drifted apart, friction being caused partly by the continued residence in England of Bordeaux, who had been accredited to the Commonwealth, partly owing to the intrigues of Henrietta Maria, who worked with the aid of France to overthrow Hyde, the English Chancellor, her declared enemy. It was not until Bordeaux had been recalled, the triumph of Hyde assured, and the marriage of the English Princess Henrietta with Louis XIY.'s brother carried out in March 1661, that all danger of hostilities was averted.

From May 29, 1660, the date of the Restoration, to the end of the year Mazarin, among his other anxieties, had to face the possibility of a rupture with England. Charles II. opened the ball by refusing to receive Bordeaux, whom he accused of favouring the Commonwealth and of attempting to influence Monk against a restoration. In July Bordeaux left England, and Charles, realising that a war at that moment might shake his throne, made secret overtures to Louis XIV. and Mazarin.

The latter, anxious to leave France at peace, accepted Charles's excuses, and the Count of Soissons was sent with great ceremony to congratulate Charles on his accession. A proposal that Charles should marry Hortensia Mancini was swept aside by the cardinal, who thus a second time declined to allow one of his nieces to marry a king. On the contrary, he encouraged the project of a marriage between Charles and Katharine of Braganza. By one of the articles of the Treaty of the Pyrenees, France had engaged not to aid Portugal in her struggle for independence against Spain, either directly or indirectly. It was very doubtful if Portugal unaided could hold her own against the Spanish armies, and in bringing about a marriage between Charles IL and Katharine of Braganza the French government was securing for Portugal a valuable ally. Since 1660 the relations between England and Portugal had been almost uniformly friendly. It was not, however, till 1662 that the marriage took place. In February 1661, shortly before Mazarin's death, Henrietta, Charles II.'s sister, arrived in France for her marriage with Philip, Duke of Anjou, and later Duke of Orleans. This marriage which was celebrated on March 31, had Mazarin's full approbation. It removed all causes of irritation between England and

France, and led to a close alliance between the two countries. Till William III.'s accession France gained enormously by this alliance. England never interfered seriously or for any prolonged period with the schemes of Louis XIV., Dunkirk was recovered, and the wisdom which guided all Mazarin's relations with England was again fully exemplified.

MAZARIN'S DEATH, CHARACTER, AND WORK

Though not yet sixty years of age, on his return to Paris in August 1660 Mazarin was an old man. In spite, however, of the gout and other infirmities, he never displayed more energy and activity than during the last years of his life. He carefully watched over the execution of the terms of the Peace of Westphalia, he contributed to the peace of the north by the Treaties of Copenhagen and Oliva, he maintained peace between France and

England during a most critical period, and he brought to a conclusion most advantageous to France the Peace of the Pyrenees. During the autumn of the year 1660 he lived first in the Louvre, where Molière's plays *L'Étourdi* and the *Précieuses ridicules* were performed before him, and in November he moved to Vincennes. In January 1661 he was again at the Louvre, where on February 6 he narrowly escaped being the victim of a fire, which broke out through the carelessness of a workman, and in which many valuable pictures and tapestries were destroyed. He then moved to his own palace in the Rue Richelieu, where he was warned by his physician, Guénant, that his end was near. It was at this period that occurred the scene rendered famous by the account of an eye-witness, the Count of Brienne, who was hid behind the arras. Determined to take a last farewell of his treasures, the cardinal, in his fur-lined dressing-gown, stole into his picture-galleries, and dragged himself feebly and wearily along. At each step his weakness forced him to stop, and Brienne heard him murmur, "Il faut quitter tout cela." As he went on he repeated, as he gazed first on one object and then on another: "Il faut quitter tout cela." M. Chéruel throws doubt on the truth of the above story, as Brienne's memoirs are for the most part inaccurate. Such a scene, however, might well have taken place, for Mazarin's love of his Correggios, Titians, and Caraccis is well known, and to desire to see his favourite pictures was only natural. He now left the noise and bustle of the Palais Mazarin for the quiet of Vincennes, and on February 28 was able to sign the treaty with the Duke of Lorraine. It was about this time that he gave his famous last injunctions to Louis XIV. He counselled the king only to choose for church preferment men who were capable, pious, and loyal; to treat the nobles and magistrates well, though the latter should not be allowed to go beyond their regular duties ; and especially to relieve the wants of the common people. Above all, he insisted on the necessity of the king governing without the aid of a First Minister. While recommending le Tellier and Lionne as faithful servants, Mazarin indicated Colbert as the man most suitable to preside over the management of the finances. The king should preside over the Council, and there should be no First Minister. On Louis XIV.'s refusal to accept all his fortune, Mazarin made a will leaving it to his relations. Charles-Armand de la Porte, son of the Marshal de la Meilleraye, who had married Hortensia Mancini on

February 28, 1661, was authorised to take the title of Duke of Mazarin, and received a large portion of the cardinal's money and property, including the palace in Paris, the duchies of Mayenne and Rethelois, and, if the king permitted, the governments of Alsace and Brouage. The rest was divided amongst his Mancini and Martinozzi nieces, and his nephew, Philip Mancini, who also received his palace at Rome and the duchies of Nevers and Donziais. Besides his legacies to his relations, Mazarin left bequests to the king, Anne of Austria, the young queen, and the Duke of Anjou. He also left donations for certain hospitals and convents. All his papers were placed in the hands of Colbert, and have been for the most part carefully preserved. On March 9, 1661, Mazarin died, and was buried first in the chapel at Vincennes, and later, in accordance with his own wish, in the chapel belonging to the College of the Quatre Nations. The French Revolutionists, in order to show their contempt for the glorious history of their country, scattered the ashes of the cardinal, whose tomb is, however, preserved in the Louvre.

Mazarin had certainly deserved well of France. At the time of the Fronde the country was torn by civil war, invaded by the Spaniards, exploited by the nobles. Many provinces were in revolt, and the central authority was practically non-existent. While the *parlement* drove Mazarin into exile, some of its partisans were in treasonable correspondence with Spain. In 1653, supported by the *bourgeoisie,* Mazarin had succeeded in establishing the royal authority on a firm basis. He then set himself to recover for France that position in Europe which the Fronde troubles had for a time destroyed. In 1661 France had, thanks to Mazarin's alliance with Oliver Cromwell, triumphed over Spain, and before the car-dinal's death the way was prepared for the continuance of friendly relations with the restored English monarchy. In 1661 France stood forth the first power in Europe. Spain was rapidly declining. Italy was divided among numerous separate states, some of which, such as Modena, Mantua, and Savoy, were allies of France. In 1661, too, thanks to Mazarin's care, Cosmo dei Medicis, the son of the Grand Duke of Tuscany, married Marguerite-Louise of Orleans, and France gained a valuable Italian ally. Closely connected by bonds of friendship with Sweden and the members of the League of the Rhine, France had nothing to fear from Germany when Mazarin's diplomacy had reduced the Emperor's power and prestige. Holland alone was, not unnaturally, actuated by a hostile and suspicious spirit. But Mazarin's diplomacy had left the Dutch helpless and without allies, to await the famous onslaught of Louis XIV. in 1672.

Though he had failed in one of the principal objects of his earlier foreign policy—the annexation of the Spanish Low Countries—he had by the marriage treaty between Louis XIV. and the Spanish Infanta prepared the way for future efforts in that direction. The German members of the League of the Rhine had also bound themselves not to permit the passage through their territories of any troops destined for the Spanish Netherlands. Mazarin had thus done all in his power to counteract the famous check which his diplomacy received in January 1648, when Holland made her alliance with Spain. A satisfactory balance of power had been established in Central and Northern Europe by the Treaties of Westphalia, Pyrenees, and Oliva, and France, triumphant over both branches of the house of Hapsburg, was regarded as the protector of the rights and liberties of the German princes. In 1661, then, France held a position of incontestable superiority in Europe. This position was due to the consummate diplomatic àkill of Mazarin, supplemented by the marvellous military talents of Turenne and by the genius and trustworthiness of his agents, especially of Lionne, Servien, and le Tellier.

The question frequently presents itself, as one follows the fortunes of Mazarin and watches the effects of his policy, what would Richelieu have done under similar circumstances? That the internal troubles in France would never have developed into the movement of the First Fronde under Richelieu's hands may be taken for granted. But it must be remembered that Richelieu had years of experience in official life before he was called upon to undertake the duties of First Minister.

Mazarin was, during the early years of his ministry, hampered and opposed in every possible way, and instead of being supported, like Richelieu, by a king, he had to govern the country on behalf of a woman and a child. During the troubles and civil wars which occupied France from 1648 to 1653, it is impossible not to admire the skill shown by the Italian cardinal, and the way in which " though twice fallen and exiled, he speedily climbed up again with a cheerful and dauntless spirit." With the aid of Condé he vanquished the First or

Parliamentary Fronde, and the Peace of Rueil was concluded. But the pride and ambition of Condé, backed up by the *petits-maîtres,* led to fresh difficulties. Condé insulted the queen and Mazarin, and aimed at making himself all-powerful. To check Condé's designs and to preserve the monarchy, Mazarin then allied with the leading members of the First Fronde ; and Condé, Conti, and Longueville were imprisoned. He then suppressed disorder in Normandy, Burgundy, and Guienne, and defeated the Spaniards in the battle of Rethel. These successes, one would have expected, would have strengthened Mazarin's position. The very reverse happened. Thinking himself able to overcome all his enemies, Mazarin treated the powerful de Retz with contempt, and took no steps to nullify intrigues or to avert open attacks. The union of Orleans and the members of the First Fronde with the princes who composed the Second or New Fronde upset all his calculations, and he was compelled to leave France. From Brühl, however, he directed with infinite skill the policy, of the queen. The union of the two Frondes soon broke up. Between the ambition of Condé and the indolence of Orleans there was nothing in common Condé, unconciliatory and rash to the end, refused, when

Louis XIV.'s majority was declared, to lay down his ambitions, and plunged into rebellion. From this moment, when the country rallied round the king as the impersonation of the national greatness, Mazarin's fortunes improved. Gradually a complete revolution in public opinion was effected, and men realised the selfishness and want of patriotism of Condé and his followers. Supported by the *bourgeoisie* and by all those who preferred the interests of France to the triumph of a faction, and always using bribery to gain over the nobles and others, Mazarin brought about the ruin of both Frondes, and enabled the monarchy to prepare for a successful struggle against its internal foes.

That struggle was practically closed with the capitulation of Bordeaux in 1653, and during the ensuing years Mazarin, supported by the energetic young king, reduced the *parlement* of Paris to submission. The administrative system erected by Richelieu had withstood the attacks of both nobles and *parlement,* and was again set in motion. From the *Conseil du Roi,* or Council of the King, had been formed the Council of State, in which the ministers sat. Wielding, under the crown, enormous powers, the Council was supreme over the law courts and over all administrative bodies. The ministers could only advise, for all power rested ultimately with the king. The Fronde troubles had shown the incapacity both of the *parlement* of Paris and of the nobles to govern the kingdom. It was better that France should be under a monarchy than ruled by a narrow, selfish bureaucracy or by an anarchic, feudal aristocracy.

Mazarin's character has been the subject of much adverse criticism. The fact that he was an Italian rendered his position as First Minister in France always difficult, and made attacks on him popular. The language adopted towards him in the Mazarinades and by such men as de Retz was bitter in the extreme. Later writers, recognising the magnitude of his statesmanlike services to France, have awarded him fairer treatment. The Due d'Aumale, in his admirable work on *The Princes of the House of Condé,* has noted some of the characteristics of Mazarin's complex character. "A great, gambler, a scorner of danger, too greedy to be a good administrator … he has views on foreign affairs, on diplomacy and war, the full extent of which cannot be derived from his despatches." He then notices Mazarin's "submissive language, his studied obscurity, his repetitions, his contradictions," extols his skill in negotiations, and declares that "an habitual craftiness led him too often astray in his relations with his fellow-men." M. Chéruel, in his *Histoire de France pendant la minorité de Louis XIV.,* sums up in an admirable manner the striking points in the cardinal's complex character. He draws special attention to his knowledge of European affairs, to his sagacity and presence of mind when unravelling the most complicated intrigues, to his perseverance, and to his patience and foresight in waiting for favourable opportunities for the execution of his plans. His indomitable ardour for work is proved by his voluminous correspondence. "Unfortunately, cunning, duplicity, and a sordid avarice were a serious drawback to Mazarin's good qualities." Mazarin's greatness was undoubted, though few of his contemporaries realised it. His correspondence contains ample proof of his statesmanlike qualities, and of his determination to place the country of his adoption at the head of European nations. Having attained this object of his ambition and perseverance, he is worthy to be ranked with Richelieu as a great minister. As a diplomatist he was unequalled. Sweden and Savoy were among his most faithful allies. When deserted by the Dutch he formed an alliance with England, with the happiest results for France. By the Peace of Westphalia he prepared the way for the League of the Rhine, and by the Peace of the Pyrenees for the absorption by France of a portion of the Spanish Netherlands. Never during the troubled years of the Fronde did his indefatigable activity cease or his perseverance give way to despair. Contemporary writers were, however, usually impressed by the faults of his character, by his intrigues and underhand methods of obtaining his ends, by his spy system and his avarice. Rarely has a great minister afforded to hostile pamphleteers so many opportunities for attack, and the Mazarinades show how ably his enemies took advantage of the defects of his character. They could not appreciate the value to France of the Peace of Westphalia; they had no wish to praise Mazarin's prudence, sagacity, and perseverance.

Though not fitted by nature to crush and destroy the nobles as Richelieu would have done, Mazarin's patience and flexibility proved equal to the task left him by his predecessor. "Mazarin," it has been said, "had a bold heart and weaker mind ; Richelieu a daring mind and timid heart." Gentle and unassuming in demeanour, Mazarin was full of kindness and readily accessible to all comers. Above the middle height, he was one of the handsomest men at the court. His hair was auburn,his forehead broad, his nose large, his beard carefully curled, his hands small and well formed. Like the queen-regent, to whom he was married, few who came into contact with him could resist the fascination of the good-looking cardinal. His mind was more subtle than that of Richelieu, and Italian-like he preferred the refinements of intrigue to a more strenuous and resolute policy. Instead of attempting to break his opponents, he consistently endeavoured to bend them to adopt his views. A well-educated man, his interest in art and literature was remarkable. In 1646 he bought the Hôtel Tuboeuf, on the site of which now stands the "Bibliothèque Nationale," and built the Palais Mazarin. During the rest of his life he took every opportunity of enriching his palace with works of art, tapestry, and with all materials beautiful in design. Clarendon tells us that, after the death of Charles I., Mazarin bought "rich goods and jewels of the rifled crown, of which he purchased the rich beds, hangings, and carpets which furnished his palace in Paris." Though he missed the chance of buying Raphael's cartoons, he enriched, his galleries with many valuable pictures collected from all parts of Europe. His tapestry had a worldwide fame, and though it was temporarily dispersed in 1651 by order of the *parlement* of Paris, it was restored to him later. Mazarin was perhaps the best-dressed man of his day, and his wardrobe was remarkable for the number and richness of the suits which it contained. A born virtuoso, his cabinets contained many priceless jewels and other masterpieces of the goldsmith's art.

The enumeration of articles "in rock-crystal, amber, coral, and other precious materials, enchâssées dans l'argent vermeil doré,'" fill twenty-two pages of the *Inventaire de tous les meubles de Cardinal Mazarin,* drawn up in 1653 and edited in 1661 by the Due d'Aumale. In the same work will be found lists of his furniture and a catalogue of his gilt and silver plate.

He was also a patron of literature and a lover of books. The great age of French literature was dawning, and he pensioned Balzac, Voiture, Descartes, Chapelain, Corneille, Bossuet, Pascal, Molière, Racine, Boileau, Madame de Sévigné, and many other writers who adorned the golden period of French literature, and who, now that order was re-established and that patriotism had conquered, were beginning to write. The movement in literary as in political history which is summed up in the term " The Age of Louis XIV. " was fostered by

Mazarin, who founded the Collège Mazarin, which afterwards became the Institut of France, introduced the opera, and supported the drama. Having secured in Naudé a competent librarian, Mazarin, like his contemporary Cardinal Francesco Barberini, who collected a splendid library, before the end of 1648 had acquired some 40,000 volumes, which he placed in his library for the use of the learned and for students. Naudé had traversed all Europe, in his own words visiting " Flanders, Italy, England, and Germany, to bring hither whatever is rare and excellent." By great good fortune this library escaped destruction in 1649, and again in 1651, when it fell into the power of the *parlement.* That body was willing to please the vandalism of the populace by attacks on the Palais Mazarin and its treasures.

Though all his collections were dispersed, his library-escaped, and his books now form the Bibliothèque Mazarine, which is in the buildings of the Institut.

Though Mazarin amassed an enormous fortune, he seems to have been ignorant of financial matters. Like Eichelieu, he did nothing to reform the financial administration of France. Both cardinals failed as economists, and it was left to Colbert to carry on the work of Sully. During Mazarin's lifetime the privileged classes were exempt from the oppressive direct taxes, and the indirect taxes were assessed most unequally and unjustly. Emery, Mazarin's first *contrôleur-général,* was, like Calonne, skilful in staving off immediate difficulties and in obtaining money for the time. The sale of offices continued, and the practice of farming the indirect taxes was confirmed. The government thus was placed at the mercy of the financiers, who assessed and recovered the taxes, and who made immense fortunes out of the taxpayers. Early in 1647 the State was practically bankrupt. Emery's *édit du toisé* had been withdrawn, and the *taxe des aisés* and the *édit du tarif* yielded little. Among the causes of the opposition to Mazarin, irritation at the conduct of the farmers of the taxes was not the least. From 1652 to 1660 Mazarin found Fouquet invaluable for procuring loans for the State, while his selection of Colbert to manage his private affairs was an act the wisdom of which cannot be over-estimated. Colbert fully justified the cardinal's confidence in his honesty and financial ability. The Brouage property which belonged to Mazarin was well managed, and proved a valuable source of income, and Colbert's efforts after economy were seconded by his master. Mazarin's correspondence with Colbert gives many, proofs not only of Mazarin's avaricious nature, but also of his business-like way of looking at money. He had, it is often said, the instincts of a trader. Like Walpole in the next century, Mazarin was well aware of the value of money in politics. Throughout the Fronde troubles enormous sums were spent in buying important politicians, and during his negotiations with the German princes at the time of the Emperor Leopold's election, the bribery of the electors and others was on a large scale. It must always be remembered that Mazarin, at critical moments in the history of France, was always ready to employ his wealth for the public good. During the German negotiations in 1657, the Treasury being well-nigh empty, he advanced the necessary funds, and on his death-bed he offered to leave his riches to Louis XIV. Over his avarice, which was greaty his patriotism always triumphed. He is often criticised for handing over the finances to the care of Fouquet, of whose methods he was well aware. But it was not easy to see from what other quarter during the later years of Mazarin's life money could have been obtained. Moreover, Colbert, like a watch-dog, was continually on the alert. While he reorganised Mazarin's own estate with such success that Mazarin rapidly accumulated an immense fortune, he declared war upon Fouquet. Envious, alert, and capable, Colbert never ceased from 1653 to observe every action of Fouquet, and to note every suspicious circumstance. But Mazarin wisely continued till his death to employ the magnificent Fouquet, whose credit with financiers had been so invaluable to him during the stormy period from which he emerged in 1659. Though he sought for no opportunity of improving the internal wellbeing of France to a material extent, he at any rate bequeathed Colbert to Louis XIV.

In advising Louis to employ Colbert, Mazarin gave another illustration of his skill in choosing subordinates and his preference for the *bourgeois* class. Le Tellier, a hard-working, prudent man, Servien and Lionne, able diplomatists, and Colbert, a skilled economist, were all men belonging to the *bourgeoisie,* and were all trained in the service of the cardinal. In 1643 le Tellier was placed at the head of the war department, and carried out his duties with vigour and diligence. He aided in bringing about the Treaty of Rueil, and during the absence of the court from Paris in 1650 he was specially entrusted to watch Orleans and to report to Mazarin. During Mazarin's exile in 1651 le Tellier, with Servien and Lionne, remained, with the exception of one short period, in Paris, aiding Anne of Austria, watching Orleans, and corresponding with Mazarin. On Mazarin's second exile le Tellier was entrusted with the management of all the State business, and till the cardinal's return was practically the head of the government. An astute, avaricious man, le Tellier was admirably fitted to occupy a high place in the State. Till 1666 he remained at the head of the war department, which he then resigned in favour of his son-in-law Louvois. Servien, the uncle of Lionne, had characteristics very different from those of le Tellier. While the latter was insinuating in his manners, and preferred the byways of intrigue in order to attain his object, the former was straightforward and irascible.

His direct methods proved useful in the negotiations immediately preceding the conclusion of the Peace of Westphalia, and Mazarin showed his appreciation of his merits by making him a secretary of state, and in 1652 joint superintendent of the finances with Fouquet. Always haughty and severe, Servien was a striking contrast to the corrupt and immoral nobles and officials by whom he was surrounded. He had little in common with Fouquet, and Mazarin in 1654 acted wisely in dividing their functions. He died in 1659, leaving France successful abroad and the work begun at Westphalia on the verge of completion.

Lionne is a more interesting figure than either le Tellier or Servien. During the stormy times of the Second Fronde he played an important part as one of Mazarin's principal subordinates in Paris. But it was as an ambassador that Lionne is most celebrated. He was entrusted by Mazarin with the difficult task of arranging matters with the papacy in connection with de Retz's claim to the Archbishopric of Paris ; he took a leading part in organising the League of the Rhine, and in making the Treaty of the Pyrenees. Louis XIV. found his diplomatic skill of great use during the early part of his reign. Striking as were the diplomatic qualities of Lionne, they were destined to prove less remarkable than the financial skill of Colbert. But while Lionne's most celebrated successes belong to Mazarin's ministry, Colbert's career as a reformer and economist did not begin till after the cardinal's death. During the last nine years of Mazarin's life Colbert was constantly by his side. Colbert, like Turenne, always advocated a direct, vigorous policy. Like Richelieu he desired the adoption of firm measures with the *parlement,* and of stern methods towards all who resisted the king's authority. Though ambitious and often over-severe and unjust in his decisions, Colbert was admirably fitted for the task of reorganising the finances of France. His jealousy of Fouquet was natural, and a struggle between the two systems of finance as represented by the two men was inevitable. Aided by these able subordinates, Mazarin, after the conclusion of the Fronde troubles, began the work of reorganisation.

First in importance was the re-establishment of the intendants. Eichelieu had made the intendants permanent officials with wide powers, which extended over the whole kingdom, of justice, police, and finance. As the recognised channel of communication between the country districts and the royal Council, they at once roused the jealousy of the privileged classes, and one of the principal objects of the early Frondeurs was to procure their abolition. Though the nobles continued to derive their revenues from the provinces of which they were nominal governors, all real control over the provincial administration passed into the hands of the intendants, who, being middle-class officials, had not the ambition of the noble orders. Mazarin thus continued and developed Eichelieu's policy of making the intendants the basis of a powerful monarchical system. Under Louis XIV. these agents proved efficient ; it was not till the following century that the evils of over-centralisation became apparent. Equally effective had been Mazarin's treatment of the *parlement* of Paris. Its claim to be superior to the States-General was heard no more ; its attempt to wield political power was pushed aside. Its eminent president Molé had, till his resignation in 1653, endeavoured with some success to induce it to adhere to the terms of the famous royal declaration of October 22, 1652, though his successor, Pomponne de Bellièvre, in 1655 had attempted, but in vain, to regain for the *parlement* a recognition of its possession of political power. In 1657 the discontent of the *parlement* had been again allayed by a mixture of firmness and adroitness on Mazarin's part. When he died the cardinal had reason to expect fresh opposition from the *parlement* to the royal will, but Louis XIV. soon made it apparent that no resistance on its part would be brooked.

During the minority of Louis XIII. the *parlement* had asserted its right to be heard, but in 1641 Richelieu had issued an edict forbidding that body to take any cognis-ance of affairs of State. Its political power had thus been summarily suppressed, and it was ordered that all edicts were to be registered at once. Taking advantage of the irresolute rule of Anne of Austria, and of the consequent troubles of the Fronde period, the *parlement* regained its former position. But its triumph was only temporary, and it was not till the minority of Louis XV. that it again asserted its right to interfere in State affairs, and to represent the nation.

During the years succeeding 1653 Mazarin showed no interest in improving the internal organisation of France, or in developing the natural wealth and resources of the country. He neglected agriculture, commerce, manufactures, and the colonies. "If Cardinal Mazarin," writes Colbert, "understood foreign affairs, he was utterly ignorant of home government." Though by his foreign policy he had raised France to a great height of glory, he does not seem to have understood the meaning and value of good government. During the eight years following the close of the Fronde attempts were indeed made to improve the condition of French commerce. Mazarin took no sustained interest in the prosperity of trade or of the navy. In his later years, however, he was well served by Colbert, who urged the importance of measures for the development of trade, agriculture, and manufactures. Years had, however, to elapse before France could recover from the effects of the dislocation of her industrial life caused by her foreign wars and domestic troubles. Nevertheless, it was during Mazarin's ministry that Colbert made his first efforts towards that striking colonial, commercial, and manufacturing expansion which marked the first decade of Louis XIV.'s personal rule.

In 1661 Mazarin had restored order in France, but he was well aware of the importance of leaving the country in the hands of a firm ruler who would continue his policy. During the years between 1653 and 1661 he had paid considerable attention to the political and military education of the young king. In 1653 Louis for the first time had accompanied Turenne on a campaign. From that year, too, he was constantly with Mazarin, imbibing principles of conduct which he afterwards drew up for the instruction of his own son. Mazarin taught him to work hard, to learn self-control, to accept advice from his generals and ministers. Owing to Mazarin's counsels, Louis, though remaining ignorant in literary matters, learnt to rule men, and, like Mazarin, to pursue with perseverance the objects of his policy. "It will depend entirely on yourself," Mazarin once said to the king, " to become the most glorious king that has ever lived. God has given you all the necessary qualities, and all you have to do is to employ them." Mazarin's expectations were not disappointed, and his constant care for Louis' education was amply rewarded. In 1654 Louis was present at the siege of Stenay, and in 1655 the firmness of his character was well exemplified in his treatment of the *parlement* of Paris. There is no doubt that Louis benefited immensely by his experience of camp life during the later phases of the Spanish war, and the lessons on the political state of Europe which he constantly received from Mazarin. On his death-bed the cardinal, in giving Louis good advice as to his treatment of his subjects, urged him to be absolute and not to govern through others. The fate of Fouquet, shortly after Mazarin's death, was an immediate and conclusive proof that Louis intended to carry out his late minister's final injunctions.

Mazarin's defects are obvious to the student of the Fronde period, but it is impossible to deny his consistent patriotism or the immense services which he rendered to France. He carried out the policy of Henry IY. and

Richelieu, and permanently weakened both branches of the house of Hapsburg. At the Peace of AYestphalia the Emperor was forced to grant independence, religious and political, to the German princes, and France gained Alsace, Brisach, and Philipsburg. The Peace of the Pyrenees signified the fall of the Spanish Hapsburgs from the high position which they had held in Europe since the days of Ferdinand and Isabella, and by that peace France secured Artois, Roussillon, and a portion of Flanders. The Fronde had unmistakably proved that monarchy was the only form of government suitable for or possible in France. Mazarin had steadily persevered in his task of curbing the *parlement* and of reducing the ambition of the nobles. Having assured the triumph of the monarchy, he spent the last eight years of his life in strengthening its position at home and abroad. The debt of France to Mazarin is immense. Like Disraeli he made his adopted country his first thought, and like Disraeli he eventually overcame the hostility caused by his foreign extraction. But while the English minister was not only a man of genius but also a man of action, and often delighted in dramatic *coups,* Mazarin was not a man of genius, but a diplomatist of the first order.

IMPORTANT DATES

1642   Dec.   5. Death of Richelieu.

1643   May 14. Death of Louis XIII. ; Accession of Louis XIV.

May 18. Mazarin confirmed as First Minister. May 19. Battle of Rocroi. Sept. 2. Overthrow of the *Importants.* Nov. 24. Battle of Diittlingen.

1644   Jan. 27. Edict of the *toisé.*

Apr. 10. Congress opened at Miinster. Aug. 3, 5, 9. Battle of Freiburg. Sept. 15. Innocent X. elected Pope.

1645   March.   Reimposition of the *toisé* tax. May 5. Battle of Mergentheim. Aug. 3. Battle of Nördlingen.

Aug. 14. Treaty of Brömsebro.

Sept. 7. A *lit de justice* ; the *parlement* submissive.

Nov. 25. Treaty between France and Denmark.

1646   June 14. Naval battle off Orbitello. July. Belliévre sent to England. Oct.   9. Capture of Piombino.

Oct. 11. Capture of Dunkirk by Enghien. Oct. 29. Capture of Porto Longone. Nov. 21. Harcourt raises the siege of Lérida. Dec. 26. Enghien becomes Prince of Condé on the death of his father. 179

1647   Mar. 14. The Treaty of Ulm.

June 17. The siege of Lérida is raised by Condé.

July   7. Revolt of Masaniello.

Oct. 24. A republic proclaimed in Naples.

1648   January. Treaty between Spain and the United Provinces.

May 13. The *parlement* and the Sovereign Courts

unite.

May 17. Battle of Zusmarshausen.

July 13. Tortosa is taken.

July 26. Little Prague is taken.

Ang. 20. Battle of Lens.

Aug. 26. A *coup d'état* is carried out.

Oct. 22. Declaration of Saint-Germain.

Oct. 24. Peace of Westphalia.

1649. Jan. 5. The court leaves Paris. Outbreak of Civil

War.

Jan.-Mar. Siege of Paris. Apr. 2. Treaty of Rueil. Aug. 18. Return of the court to Paris.

1650. Jan. 18. Arrest of the three princes. Feb. 1-21. The court in Normandy. . 11. Capture of Bellegarde. July 16. The court arrives at Tours. August. Piombino and Porto Longone retaken by

Spain.

Aug. 29. The three princes removed to Marcoussis. Sept. 29. Bordeaux capitulates. Nov. 6. Death of the Stadtholder William II. Nov. 8. The court at Fontainebleau. Nov. 25. The three princes removed to Havre. Dec. 15. Battle of Rethel. Dec. 31. Mazarin arrives in Paris.

1651 Feb. 6. Release of the princes. March. First

exile of Mazarin.

Sept. 7. Louis XIV. attains his majority.

Oct.-Dec. Civil war in Saintonge. Oct. 31. The court at Poitiers.

1652   Jan. 29. Mazarin joins the court at Poitiers.Mar. 28. Battle of Jargeau.

April 7. Battle of Bléneau.

May 4. Battle of Étampes.

July 2. Battle of Saint-Antoine.

Aug. 6. The *parlement* at Pontoise.

Aug. 19. Second exile of Mazarin.

Sept. 16. Capture of Dunkirk by the Spaniards.

Oct. 21. Return of the king and court to Paris.

1653   Feb. 3. Return of Mazarin to Paris.

July 31. Submission of Bordeaux and end of the Provincial Fronde.

1654   Feb. 22. Marriage of Conti with a niece of Mazarin. May 21. Treaty of Basle with Harcourt.

June 7. Coronation of Louis XIV. at Rheims. Aug. 5. Capture of Stenay. Aug.   8. Escape of de Retz.

1655   Nov. 3. Treaty of Westminster between France and

England.

1656   Jan.   3. Death of Molé.

Aug. 18. Capture of the town of Condé by Spain.

1657   Mar. 23. Treaty of Paris between England and France. April 1. Death of the Emperor Ferdinand.

Oct.   3. Mardyke is taken and given to England.

1658   Mar. 28. The Franco-English alliance is renewed. June 14. Battle of the Dunes.

June 18. Election of the Emperor Leopold.

June 25. Capture of Dunkirk.

Aug. 14. The League of the Rhine is formed.

Sept. 3. Death of Cromwell.

Nov.   The king and court at Lyons.

1659   Jan. 28. The king and court at Paris.

May 8. An armistice between France and Spain. Oct. 14-Dec. 27. The king and court at Toulouse. Nov. 7. The Peace of the Pyrenees.

1660.   Jan.-Mar. Louis XIV. in Provence. May   3. The Treaty of Oliva. May 29. Restoration of Charles II. June 6. The Treaty of Copenhagen. June 9. Marriage of Louis XIV. with the Spanish Infanta.

1661.   Feb. 28. Treaty with Lorraine. Mar. 9. Death of Mazarin.

Printed in Great Britain
by Amazon